YANN MARTEL

—

WHAT IS STEPHEN HARPER READING?

—

YANN MARTEL'S
RECOMMENDED READING
for a
PRIME MINISTER
and
BOOK LOVERS OF ALL STRIPES

VINTAGE CANADA

VINTAGE CANADA EDITION, 2009

Copyright © 2009 Yann Martel

Published in Canada by Vintage Canada, a division of Random House of Canada Limited, Toronto, in 2009. Distributed by Random House of Canada Limited, Toronto.

Vintage Canada with colophon is a registered trademark.

www.randomhouse.ca

Pages 229 to 230 constitute a continuation of the copyright page.

LIBRARY AND ARCHIVES CANADA CATALOGUING IN PUBLICATION

Martel, Yann
What is Stephen Harper reading? : Yann Martel's recommended reading for a prime minister (and book lovers of all stripes) / Yann Martel.

ISBN 978-0-307-39867-3

1. Best books. 2. Martel, Yann—Books and reading. 3. Martel, Yann—Correspondence. 4. Harper, Stephen, 1959–   . I. Title.

Z1035.9.M37 2009   011'.73   C2009-902614-7

Printed and bound in the United States of America

2 4 6 8 9 7 5 3 1

To Alice, my favourite reader

CONTENTS

This is a book about books. It takes the form of a series of letters. The letters were written by a Canadian writer—me—and sent to a Canadian politician, Prime Minister Stephen Harper. In each letter I discuss a literary work, be it a novel, a play, a poetry collection, a religious text, a graphic novel, a children's book, and so on—the range is wide. I mailed a copy of each work, dated, numbered and inscribed, with the accompanying letter neatly folded inside its front cover, to the Prime Minister's Office in Ottawa. Politely and unfailingly, I have been doing this every two weeks since April 16, 2007, and the project is ongoing. The purpose was and is to remind Stephen Harper of the life-shaping marvel contained within books.

So far, I have received two replies. The first came promptly:

May 8, 2007

Dear Mr. Martel:

On behalf of the Prime Minister, I would like to thank you for your recent letter and the copy of Tolstoy's *The Death of Ivan Ilych*. We appreciated reading your comments and suggestions regarding the novel.

Once again, thank you for taking the time to write.

Sincerely,
Susan I. Ross
Assistant to the Prime Minister

A long, official silence of nearly two years followed. Then, unexpectedly, I received a reply for the fifty-third and fifty-fourth books I had sent:

April 29, 2009

Dear Mr. Martel,

On behalf of the Right Honourable Stephen Harper, I would like to acknowledge receipt of your correspondence, with which you enclosed a copy of *The Sailor Who Fell from Grace with the Sea* by Yukio Mishima and a copy of *Louis Riel, A Comic-Strip Biography* by Chester Brown.

The Prime Minister wishes me to convey his thanks for sending him these books. You may be assured that your thoughtful gesture is most appreciated.

Yours truly,
S. Russell
Executive Correspondence Officer

It's been a lonely book club. I started it in a moment of frustration. In late March 2007 I was invited to Ottawa to help celebrate the fiftieth anniversary of the Canada Council for the Arts, that towering institution that has done so much to foster the cultural identity of Canadians. The celebrations turned out to be a very pleasant affair, but mostly because of the fellow artists present, fifty in all, of every discipline and tendency, a rainbow of writers, painters, composers, musicians, choreographers and others, each representing one year of the Council's fifty. I was the representative for 1991, the year I received a Canada Council grant that allowed me to write my first novel,

Self. I was twenty-seven years old and the money was manna from heaven. I made those eighteen thousand dollars last a year and a half (and considering the income tax I have paid in the wake of the success of my second novel, *Life of Pi*, this initial investment by Canadian taxpayers has been well worth it, I assure you). The eldest artist there, representing 1957, was Jean-Louis Roux, great man of the theatre; the youngest was Tracee Smith, a young aboriginal hip-hop dancer and choreographer who had just received her first grant. It was a thrill to be among such a varied gaggle of creators.

The key moment of the celebrations came at 3 p.m. on March 28. We were sitting in the Visitors' Gallery of the House of Commons, waiting. To those Canadians who haven't been, I must mention that the House of Commons, and indeed Parliament Hill as a whole, is a powerfully impressive place. It's not just the size of the chamber or its ornate design and decoration. It's the symbolism of it. A large part of the history of our nation has been played out within its four walls. While a very practical venue, fitted with functional desks, powerful, selective microphones and discreet television cameras, it's also a space of dreams and visions where we Canadians have worked out who and what we want to be.

So there I was, in the House of Commons, wowed by the place, and I got to thinking about stillness. I guess the word popped into my head because the unsettling brawl of Question Period was just coming to an end. To read a book, one must be still. To watch a concert, a play, a movie, to look at a painting, one must also be still. Religion, too, makes use of stillness, notably with prayer and meditation. Gazing upon a lake in autumn or a quiet winter scene—that too lulls us into contemplative stillness. Life, it seems, favours moments of stillness to appear on the edges of our perception and whisper to us, "Here

I am. What do you think?" Then we become busy and the still-ness vanishes, but we hardly notice because we fall so easily for the delusion of busyness, whereby what keeps us busy must be important and the busier we are with it, the more important it must be. And so we work, work, work, rush, rush, rush. On occasion we say to ourselves, panting, "Gosh, life is racing by." But that's not it at all, it's the contrary: life is still. It is we who are racing by.

The moment had come. The Minister for Canadian Heritage, Bev Oda at the time, rose to her feet, acknowledged our presence and began to speak. We artists stood up, not for ourselves but for the Canada Council and what it represents. The Minister did not speak for long. In fact, she had barely started, we thought, when she finished and sat down. There was a flutter of applause and then MPs turned to other matters. We were still standing, incredulous. That was it? Fifty years of building Canada's dazzling and varied culture, done with in less than five minutes? I remember the poet Nicole Brossard laughed and shook her head as she sat down. I couldn't quite laugh.

What would the equivalent celebration of a major cultural institution have been like in France, say? It would have been a classy, flashy, year-long, exhibition-filled extravaganza, with the President of France trying to hog as much of the limelight as possible, that's what. But there's no need to go into further details. We all know how the Europeans do culture. It's sexy and impor-tant to them. The world visits Europe because it's so culturally resplendent. We, on the other hand, were standing like dolts in a public gallery, getting in the way of more important business. And the thing is, we didn't even ask to be there. We were invited.

From the shadows into which we had been cast, I focused on one man. The Prime Minister did not speak during our brief tribute. He didn't even look up. By all appearances, he didn't even know we were there. Who is this man? What makes him tick? I asked myself. No doubt he's busy. Being Prime Minister of Canada probably fills his entire, conscious consideration. But Stephen Harper must have pockets of solitude and idleness during which he contemplates life. There must be times when his thinking goes from the instrumental—how do I do this, how do I get that?—to the fundamental—why this, why that? In other words, he must have moments of stillness. And since I deal in books, reading and writing them, and since books and stillness go well together, I decided, by means of good books, to make suggestions that would inspire stillness in Stephen Harper.

Hence the months and years of reading, thinking, writing and mailing. The books are on a shelf in an office somewhere in Ottawa, I presume. The letters are in your hands.

What was I expecting in return? That the Prime Minister would read and reply as fast as I was reading and writing to him? No, I wasn't expecting that. There will always be more books one would like to read than one will have read. And thank God for that. It will be a sad day, a sign of a shrunken Earth, when someone will claim to have read every book published. But I am expecting, eventually, a response more substantial than the mechanical replies I've received so far. Isn't that what democracy is about, the accountability of our leaders? As a citizen of the arts, I have a right to know what my elected leader thinks about reading.

Here, for example, are a few imagined replies that would have addressed the core of my inquiry:

The haughty:

Dear Mr. Martel,

Napoleon did not ride into battle with a book in his hands. Politics is action. I will perhaps consider your books when I have won all my political battles.

Yours truly,
Stephen Harper

The principled:

Dear Mr. Martel,

What I do in my moments of leisure is none of your business. Furthermore, I cannot accept your gifts because they possibly place me in a position of conflict of interest in relation to Canadian writers. I have therefore instructed my staff to donate the books you have sent me to World Literacy of Canada.

Yours truly,
Stephen Harper

The sly:

Dear Mr. Martel,

I cannot thank you enough for the wonderful books you are sending me. So many hours of reading pleasure. I can't get enough. Upon reading the Tolstoy, I was deeply struck at how fragile our grip upon life is. The Orwell had me trembling at the wickedness of the corrupt, the Agatha Christie panting with suspense, the Elizabeth Smart weeping with heartbreak, and so on with each book, a roller-coaster of wild emotions. Send me more, send me more, please. I've been managing a book every three days.

Your letters are also a source of delight—but if only they weren't so short! If they were longer, more detailed, then I would truly be a contented Canadian reader.

Yours truly,
Stephen Harper

P.S. I loved Life of Pi. *But what was that strange island about? And what are you working on now?*

The practically honest:

Dear Mr. Martel,

I don't have time to read books. I get what I need to know from briefing papers and point-form summaries prepared by my staff. But after my time in office, many years from now, I hope, then I will look at books of my choice.

Yours truly,
Stephen Harper

The brutally honest:

Dear Mr. Martel,

I don't like reading. It bores me. If that bothers you, I don't care.

Yours truly,
Stephen Harper

The openly honest:

Dear Mr. Martel,

I've never been much of a reader and I've done fine that way. But last week I happened to be near the box where your books have been accumulating and I had a free minute. I looked at them. Such a variety. It occurred to me that books are like tools. Some are ploughs, some are trowels, some are hammers, some are spirit levels. Perhaps I should try my hand, I thought. I've picked two, the Bhagavad Gita *and* Maus, *which I will try to read in my spare time. That will have to do for the moment.*

Yours truly,
Stephen Harper

Any one of these would have stopped me in my tracks. Each would have answered my main question about the Prime Minister's reading habits.

What makes me think that Stephen Harper doesn't like reading? Isn't that brazenly presumptuous of me? Has he actually confessed to me that he hasn't read a novel since high school? No, he hasn't. Stephen Harper hasn't breathed a word about his reading habits either to me or to any journalist who has asked (other than to say, during the 2004 election, that his favourite book was the *Guinness Book of World Records*). What he reads now, or if he reads at all, or what he's read in the past, remains a mystery. But if I see a man fiercely beating a horse, I feel reasonably confident in concluding that he hasn't read *Black Beauty*. If Stephen Harper were shaped and informed by literary culture, if he read novels, short stories, plays and poetry, he would love them, he would defend them, he would celebrate them. He would not try to scuttle the public means of sustaining our nation's artistic culture, retreating from doing so only when it's politically expedient. If Stephen Harper is informed by literary culture or, indeed, by culture in general, it doesn't show in what he says or what he does. The elimination of the Department of Foreign Affairs' budget for arts promotion abroad, the closing down of the CBC Radio Orchestra, the skeletonizing of the CBC as a whole, the proposed exclusion of funding to Canada's small literary and arts journals: the list, sadly, goes on.

Perhaps the man beating the horse has read *Black Beauty*, but he still wants to beat it. Maybe he thinks the horse will be fine despite being beaten. He may even think it should be beaten for its own good. All the more reason to send him good books, then, in the hope of changing his mind.

But the question still nags and needs to be answered: is it anyone's business what Stephen Harper is reading, has read, or if he reads at all? Is it not rather like stamp collecting or watching hockey, an activity that resides entirely in the domain of his private life? Shortly after I started my campaign, that's exactly what someone intimated to me. Actually, he barked it in my face. He was furious. This is a gentleman I know in Saskatoon, where I live. He kept repeating that what I was doing was an objectionable "ad hominem attack." And this was no Conservative shouting at me, not at all. He also happens to be a keen reader. An ally, I expected. At home, shaken, I looked in the dictionary to see what ad hominem meant: Latin for an attack on someone's character rather than on a position or belief he or she might hold. Is asking Stephen Harper to account for his reading habits irrelevant? Worse: is it improper and dishonourable, attacking the private man rather than his public policies?

The answer is simple. As long as someone has no power over me, I don't care what they read, or if they read at all. It's not for me to judge how people should live their lives. But once someone has power over me, then, yes, their reading does matter to me, because in what they choose to read will be found what they think and what they will do. As I wrote in one of my letters to the man, if Stephen Harper hasn't read *The Death of Ivan Ilych* or any other Russian novel, if he hasn't read *Miss Julia* or any other Scandinavian play, if he hasn't read *Metamorphosis* or any other German-language novel, if he hasn't read *Waiting for Godot* or *To the Lighthouse* or any other experimental play or novel, if he hasn't read the *Meditations* of Marcus Aurelius or *The Educated Imagination* or any other philosophical inquiry, if he hasn't read *Under Milk Wood* or any other poetic prose, if he hasn't read *Their Eyes Were Watching God* or *Drown* or any other American novel, if he hasn't read *The Cellist of Sarajevo* or *The Island Means Minago* or *The Dragonfly of Chicoutimi* or any other Canadian novel, poem or play—if Stephen Harper hasn't read any of these, then what is his mind made of? How did he get his insights into the human condition? What materials went into the building of his sensibility? What is the colour, the pattern, the rhyme and reason of his imagination? These are not questions one is usually entitled to ask. The imaginative life of our fellow citizens, like their finances, is by and large none of our business. But once a citizen is elected to public office, then their finances do become our business, and politicians routinely have to account for their financial dealings. It's the same with their imaginative dealings. Once someone has power over me, I have the right to probe the nature and quality of their imagination, because their dreams may become my nightmares.

To citizens who aspire to be successful leaders, this is the simplest way I can put it: if you want to lead, you must read.

———

I haven't been quite alone in my guerrilla book campaign. An up-to-date public record of it can be found on the internet in English at www.whatisstephenharperreading.ca and in French at www.quelitstephenharper.ca. Steve Zdunich set up and maintained these blogs for me for longer than he should have. And then Dennis Duro showed me how I could run them myself. To them I am grateful for their freely given help. I must also thank my parents, Emile and Nicole, who stepped up to translate every letter into French, often with an unacceptably short deadline looming. They are true citizens of the arts, and to them I owe not only love but gratitude. If I love to read and write, it is because they showed me by example. I am also grateful to the University of Saskatchewan's English Department for providing me with the ideal office in which to work.

In the letters that follow are reflected the tastes, choices and limitations of one reader. Some books I had in mind long before I sent them. Others were suggested to me by readers across Canada and even from abroad. Some books I had already read, others were discoveries. I make no claim to being a wise or perceptive judge. My hope was and is to show my co-reader, the Prime Minister, how varied the written word can be. In my choices I've jumped across the barriers of borders and languages. I have so far, while I build a foundation to our library, mostly veered away from the Canadian and the contemporary, so that I can't be accused of foisting my friends upon my fellow club member. These letters are proof of no more than my personal but free engagement with the written word.

If there are readers who are dying to jump in, I encourage them to do so. Books, like fish, like to move about. Communities are made and then gain by sharing books. Any book club member will testify to the meaty pleasure of talking about a commonly read book with other people. So if you have a book you think Stephen Harper should read, by all means mail it to him. His address is:

THE RIGHT HONOURABLE STEPHEN HARPER
PRIME MINISTER OF CANADA
80 WELLINGTON STREET
OTTAWA ON K1A 0A2

Books make us climb higher, and I always have my hand on a book, as if on a banister. But unlike some readers I know who effortlessly bound up the stairs four steps at a time, floor after floor, never stopping to catch their breath, I creep up slowly. If there's an autobiographical character in my novel *Life of Pi*, it's not Pi, it's the sloth. To me, a good book is a rich lode of leaves and I can read only so many pages before my tummy gets full and I nod off. My banister is more of a branch and from it I hang upside down, nursing the book that is feeding my dreams. I read slowly but continuously. Otherwise I would starve.

Art is water, and just as humans are always close to water, for reasons of necessity (to drink, to wash, to flush away, to grow) as well as for reasons of pleasure (to play in, to swim in, to relax in front of, to sail upon, to suck on frozen, coloured and sweetened), so humans must always be close to art in all its incarnations, from the frivolous to the essential. Otherwise we dry up.

So this is the image I'd like to finish with, the quintessence of stillness and a visual summation of what I've been trying to convey to Prime Minister Stephen Harper with dozens of polite letters and good books: the image of a sloth hanging from a branch in a green jungle during a downpour of tropical rain. The rain is quite deafening, but the sloth does not mind; it's reviving, this cascade of water, and other plants and animals will appreciate it. The sloth, meanwhile, has a book on his chest, safely protected from the rain. He's just read a paragraph. It's a good paragraph, so he reads it again. The words have painted an image in his mind. The sloth examines it. It's a beautiful image. The sloth looks around. His branch is high up. Such a lovely view he has of the jungle. Through the rain, he can see spots of bright colours on other branches: birds. Down below, an angry jaguar races along a track, seeing nothing. The sloth turns back to his book. As he breathes a sigh of contentment, he feels that the whole jungle has breathed in and out with him. The rain continues to fall. The sloth falls asleep.

THE DEATH OF IVAN ILYCH
BY LEO TOLSTOY
April 16, 2007

To Stephen Harper,
Prime Minister of Canada,
From a Canadian writer,
With best wishes,
Yann Martel

Dear Mr. Harper,

The Death of Ivan Ilych, by Leo Tolstoy, is the first book I am
sending you. I thought at first I should send you a Canadian
work—an appropriate symbol since we are both Canadians—
but I don't want to be directed by political considerations of any
sort, and, more important, I can't think of any other work of
such brevity, hardly sixty pages, that shows so convincingly the
power and depth of great literature. *Ivan Ilych* is an indubitable
masterpiece. There is nothing showy here, no vulgarity, no pretence, no falseness, nothing that doesn't work, not a moment of
dullness, yet no cheap rush of plot either. It is the story, simple
and utterly compelling, of one man and his ordinary end.

Tolstoy's eye for detail, both physical and psychological,
is unerring. Take Schwartz. He is in dead Ivan Ilych's very
home, has spoken to his widow, but he is mainly concerned with
his game of cards that night. Or take Peter Ivanovich and his
struggle with the low pouffe and its defective springs while he
attempts to navigate an awkward conversation with Ivan Ilych's

widow. Or the widow herself, Praskovya Fedorovna, who weeps and laments before our eyes, yet without ever forgetting her self-interest, the details of her magistrate husband's pension and the hope of getting perhaps more money from the government. Or look at Ivan Ilych's dealings with his first doctor, who, Ivan Ilych notices, examines him with the same self-important airs and inner indifference that Ivan Ilych used to put on in court before an accused. Or look at the subtle delineation of the relations between Ivan Ilych and his wife—pure conjugal hell—or with his friends and colleagues, who, all of them, treat him as if they stood on a rock-solid bank while he had foolishly chosen to throw himself into a flowing river. Or look, lastly, at Ivan Ilych himself and his sad, lonely struggle.

How clearly and concisely our vain and callous ways are showed up. Effortlessly, Tolstoy examines life's shallow exteriors as well as its inner workings. And yet this pageant of folly and belated wisdom comes not like a dull moral lesson, but with all the weight, shine and freshness of real life. We see, vividly, Ivan Ilych's errors—oh, they are so clear to us, we certainly aren't making his mistakes—until one day we realize that someone is looking at us as if we were a character in *The Death of Ivan Ilych*.

That is the greatness of literature, and its paradox, that in reading about fictional others we end up reading about ourselves. Sometimes this unwitting self-examination provokes smiles of recognition, while other times, as in the case of this book, it provokes shudders of worry and denial. Either way, we are the wiser, we are existentially thicker.

One quality that you will no doubt notice is how despite the gulf of time between when the story is set—1882—and today, despite the vast cultural distance between provincial tsarist Russia and modern Canada, the story reaches us without the least awkwardness. In fact, I can't think of a story that while completely set in its time, so very, *very* Russian, so leaps from the bounds of the local to achieve universal resonance. A peasant in China, a migrant worker in Kuwait, a shepherd in Africa, an engineer in Florida, a prime minister in Ottawa—I can imagine all of them reading *The Death of Ivan Ilych* and nodding their heads.

Above all else, I recommend the character Gerasim to you. I suspect he is the character in whom we recognize ourselves the least yet whom we yearn the most to be like. We hope one day, when the time comes, to have someone like Gerasim at our side.

I know you're very busy, Mr. Harper. We're all busy. Meditating monks in their cells are busy. That's adult life, filled to the ceiling with things that need doing. (It seems only children and the elderly aren't plagued by lack of time—and notice how they enjoy their books, how their lives fill their eyes.) But every person has a space next to where they sleep, whether a patch of pavement or a fine bedside table. In that space, at night, a book can glow. And in those moments of docile wakefulness, when we begin to let go of the day, then is the perfect time to pick up a book and be someone else, somewhere else, for a few minutes, a few pages, before we fall asleep. And there are other possibilities, too. Sherwood Anderson, the American writer best known for his collection of stories *Winesburg, Ohio,* wrote his first stories while commuting by train to work. Stephen King apparently never goes to his beloved baseball games without a book that he reads during breaks. So it's a question of choice.

And I suggest you choose, just for a few minutes every day, to read *The Death of Ivan Ilych.*

Yours truly,
Yann Martel

Reply: May 8, 2007

Dear Mr. Martel:

On behalf of the Prime Minister, I would like to thank you for your recent letter and the copy of Tolstoy's *The Death of Ivan Ilych*. We appreciated reading your comments and suggestions regarding the novel.

Once again, thank you for taking the time to write.

Sincerely,
Susan I. Ross
Assistant to the Prime Minister

LEO TOLSTOY (1828–1910) was a prolific author, essayist, dramatist, philosopher and educational reformist. Born into an aristocratic Russian family, he is best known for writing realist fiction, focusing particularly on life in Russia, and is considered one of the major contributors to nineteenth-century Russian literature. His marriage to Sophia Tolstaya (Tolstoy) produced thirteen children, eight of whom survived into adulthood. Tolstoy wrote fourteen novels (two of his most famous being *Anna Karenina* and *War and Peace*), several essays and works of non-fiction, three plays and over thirty short stories.

ANIMAL FARM
BY GEORGE ORWELL
April 30, 2007

To Stephen Harper,
Prime Minister of Canada,
From a Canadian writer,
With best wishes,
Yann Martel
P.S. Happy birthday

Dear Mr. Harper,

Now that your Flames have been knocked out of the playoffs I guess you'll have more free time on your hands.

I fear that some may criticize me for the second book I am sending you, *Animal Farm*, by George Orwell. It's so well known, and it's another book by a dead white male. But there is time yet to be representative of all those who have harnessed the word to express themselves—believe me, they are varied and legion—unless you lose the next election, which would likely give you even more time to read, but not, alas, according to my suggestions.

Many of us read *Animal Farm* when we were young— perhaps you did too—and we loved it because of the animals and the wit. But it's in our more mature years that its import can better be understood.

Animal Farm has some commonalities with *The Death of Ivan Ilych*: both are short, both show the reality-changing power of great literature, and both deal with folly and illusion. But whereas *Ivan Ilych* deals with individual folly, the failure of one individual to lead an authentic life, *Animal Farm* is about collective folly. It is a political book, which won't be lost on someone in your line of business. It deals with one of the few matters on which we can all agree: the evil of tyranny. Of course a book cannot be reduced to its theme. It's in the reading that a book is great, not in what it seeks to discuss.

But I also have a personal reason for why I've chosen *Animal Farm:* I aspire to write a similar kind of book.

Animal Farm first. You will notice right away the novel's limpid and unaffected style, Orwell's hallmark. You get the impression the words just fell onto the page, as if it were the easiest, the most natural thing in the world to write such sentences and paragraphs and pages. It's not. To think clearly and to express oneself clearly are both hard work. But I'm sure you know that from working on speeches and papers.

The story is simple. The animals of Manor Farm have had enough of Farmer Jones and his exploitative ways so they rebel, throw him out, and set up a commune run according to the highest and most egalitarian principles. But there's a rotten pig named Napoleon and another one named Squealer—a good talker he—and they are the nightmare that will wreck the dream of Animal Farm, as the farm is renamed, despite the best efforts of brave Snowball, another pig, and the meek goodness of most of the farm animals.

I've always found the end of Chapter II very moving. There's the question of five pails of milk from the cows. What to do with them, now that Farmer Jones is gone and the milk won't be sold? Mix it with the mash they all eat, hints a chicken. "Never mind the milk, comrades!" cries Napoleon. "The harvest is more important. Comrade Snowball will lead the way. I shall follow in a few minutes." And so off the animals go, to bring in the harvest. And the milk? Well, " . . . in the evening it was noticed that the milk had disappeared."

With those five pails of white milk the ideal of Animal Farm, still so young, begins to die, because of Napoleon's corrupted heart. Things only get worse, as you will see.

Animal Farm is a perfect exemplar of one of the things that literature can be: portable history. A reader who knows nothing about twentieth-century history? Who has never heard of Joseph Stalin or Leon Trotsky or the October Revolution? Not a problem: *Animal Farm* will convey to that reader the essence of what happened to our neighbours across the Arctic. The perversion of an ideal, the corruption of power, the abuse of language, the wrecking of a nation—it's all there, in a scant 120 pages. And having read those pages, the reader is made wise to the ways of the politically wicked. That too is what literature can be: an inoculation.

And now the personal reason why I've sent you *Animal Farm:* the Jewish people of Europe murdered at the hands of the Nazis also need to have their history made portable. And that is what I'm trying to do with my next book. But to take the rubble of history—so many tears, so much bloodshed—and distil it into some few elegant pages, to turn horror into something light—it's no easy feat.

I offer you, then, a literary ideal of mine, besides a great read.

Yours truly,
Yann Martel

P.S. Happy birthday.

GEORGE ORWELL (1903–1950), born Eric Arthur Blair, was an English novelist, journalist, essayist, poet and literary critic. He was born in India into what he called a "lower-upper-middle class" family. He fought and was wounded in the Spanish Civil War. His two most famous works, *Animal Farm* and *1984*, reflect his signature style as well as his two largest preoccupations: his consciousness of social injustice and his opposition to totalitarianism. He is also well known for his interest in the power of language in politics and in shaping how we view the world. He died from tuberculosis at the age of forty-six.

BOOK 3

THE MURDER OF ROGER ACKROYD
BY AGATHA CHRISTIE
May 14, 2007

To Stephen Harper,
Prime Minister of Canada,
From a Canadian writer,
With best wishes,
Yann Martel

Dear Mr. Harper,

What is there not to like about Agatha Christie? Her books are a guilty pleasure; who would have thought that murder could be so delightful? I've selected *The Murder of Roger Ackroyd* for you. Hercule Poirot, the famous Belgian detective, has rather incongruously chosen to retire to the village of King's Abbot to grow vegetable marrows. But his gardening plans are upset by a shocking murder. Who could have done it? The circumstances are so peculiar. . . .

One of the great qualities of Agatha Christie (funny how she's never referred to simply as "Christie") is that ambition and talent were perfectly matched. In over eighty novels, she delivered exactly what she promised. To do that in literature requires, I think, not only talent and a sound knowledge of one's form but also a good degree of self-knowledge. The result, besides a trail of bodies, is an artistic integrity that has endeared her to generations of readers.

On page 38 I have highlighted a line on George Eliot that I

liked: "That pen that George Eliot wrote *The Mill on the Floss* with—that sort of thing—well, it's only just a pen after all. If you're really keen on George Eliot, why not get *The Mill on the Floss* in a cheap edition and read it?"

You might have noticed that I have been sending you used books. I have done this not to save money, but to make a point, which is that a used book, unlike a used car, hasn't lost any of its initial value. A good story rolls off the lot into the hands of its new reader as smoothly as the day it was written.

And there's another reason for these used paperbacks that never cost much even when new: I like the idea of holding a book that someone else has held, of eyes running over lines that have already seen the light of other eyes. That, in one image, is the community of readers, is the communion of literature.

I was in Ottawa recently and while I was there I happened to visit Laurier House, where two of your most illustrious predecessors lived and worked: Wilfrid Laurier and William Lyon Mackenzie King. It's an impressive mansion, with dark panelling, rich carpets, imposing furniture and a hidden elevator. What a perfect setting for an Agatha Christie murder mystery, I thought, which accounts for the book now in your hands.

Did you know that both Laurier and King were voracious readers? I include photographs I took of King's library, which was also where he worked, getting Canada through the Depression and the Second World War and building the foundations of our enviable social welfare system. Remarkable the range and number of books he read, including one that I love, one of the greatest books ever written, Dante's *Divine Comedy*. There was the complete Kipling, too, and all of Shakespeare. A two-volume biography of Louis Pasteur. Books on art. Shelf after shelf of the most varied histories and biographies. There were even what looked like self-help books to do with body and health. Truly a striking library. And let's not forget the piano.

Laurier, who made a country out of an independent colony, was an even more dedicated reader. His library was so extensive that King had it shipped out when he moved in, needing space for his own collection. Laurier's books are now stored at the National Archives.

A part of King's library.

How did they manage to read so much? Perhaps Laurier and King were excellent at time management. Certainly television wasn't there to inform them in part and otherwise fruitlessly devour their hours. Or was it that reading was a natural

and essential element of being a respectable, well-rounded gentleman? Was it some ingrained habit of the privileged that gave these two prime ministers permission to spend so much time reading?

Reading was perhaps a privileged activity then. But not now. In a wealthy, egalitarian country like ours, where the literacy rate is high (although some people still

And King was a musician, too.

struggle and need our help) and public libraries are just that, public, reading is no longer an elite pastime. A good book today has no class, so to speak, and it can be had by anyone. One of the marvels of where I live, the beautiful province of Saskatchewan, is that the smallest town—Hazlet, for example, population 126— has a public library. Nor need books be expensive, if you want to own one. You can get a gold mine of a used book for fifty cents. After that, all that is needed to appreciate the investment is a little pocket of time.

I bet you King hurried to bed muttering to himself, "It was Parker the butler, I'm sure of it!"

Yours truly,
Yann Martel

DAME AGATHA CHRISTIE (1890–1977), the award-winning British author referred to by some as "the Queen of Crime," is one of the bestselling authors of all time. She is known the world over for her detective novels and created two of the most iconic detectives in crime-writing history: Hercule Poirot and Miss Jane Marple. She worked as a nurse in World War I, acquiring a knowledge of poisons and illnesses that would later serve her well when writing murder mysteries. In addition to writing more than eighty novels, she wrote several plays, short stories and romances. Many of her stories have been adapted for the screen.

BOOK 4

BY GRAND CENTRAL STATION
I SAT DOWN AND WEPT
BY ELIZABETH SMART

May 28, 2007

To Stephen Harper,
Prime Minister of Canada,
From a Canadian writer,
With best wishes,
Yann Martel

Dear Mr. Harper,

And now a book to be read aloud. I believe that's the best way to read Elizabeth Smart's *By Grand Central Station I Sat Down and Wept*. Because this is a language book, a book where language is the plot, the character and the setting. There is something else, of course, the theme, and the theme here is an old eternal one: love.

So what a perfect book to read in bed at the end of the day and aloud. A book to be shared.

The links between art and life can be reductionist, but this might help you stay afloat in the wash of language: one day Elizabeth Smart read some poems in a bookshop and she fell in love—I'm tempted to say "decided to fall in love"—with the poet, who was George Barker. Good thing for George Barker, because I suspect George Barker will be remembered by posterity more for being "the poet Elizabeth Smart fell in love with" than for his poetry. Smart and George Barker eventually met, in California, and they became lovers and her essential bliss and hell began. Because George Barker was married and would have durable relations with more women than just his wife and Elizabeth Smart. The great number of children he fathered—fifteen in all, including four with Smart—might indicate that he took the consequences of love as seriously as its emotional premise, but I doubt his fathering skills were that good. I am digressing. Elizabeth Smart fell in love with George Barker, it was killing for her heart but it yielded this jewel of a book. In a way, Smart was another Dante and *By Grand Central Station* is another *Divine Comedy,* only the direction of travel is opposite: she started in heaven and made her way to hell.

So, layers of allegorical allusions and metaphorical flights, but at the core of this book is the hard diamond of a passionate love affair.

I'll leave the love affair to your own thoughts and conclusions. What can more easily be talked about is the beauty of the language. Language is the crudest form of metaphor. It is a system of refined grunts in which, by common agreement, a sound we make—say "spinach"—is agreed to represent, to mean, that green leafy thing over there that's good to eat. It makes communicating so much easier and effective, spares one constantly having to point at with bug eyes. I can just see a group of cave people fiercely bobbing their heads up and down and grunting and shouting for joy when they first came upon the idea. It was such a good idea that it spread quickly. What a thrill, involving a fair number of bruising fights, I imagine, it must have been to be the ones who were the first to look upon the world and map it over with words. Different groups of people agreed on different grunts, and that's all right. *Vive la différence.*

And so we have: spinach, épinards, espinacas, spinaci, espinafre, spinat, spenat, pinaatti, szpinak, spenót, ШПИНАТ, السبانخ, and we are the better for it. Because these utilitarian grunts unexpectedly became a world unto themselves, offering their own possibilities. We thought language would be a simple tool directly relaying the world to us. But, lo, we found that the tool has become its own world, still relaying the outer world but in a mediated way. Now there is the word and there is the world and the two are enthralled with each other, like two lovers.

The lovers in the novel were arrested for trying to cross a state border—illicit love being a customs offence at the time—and the first pages of Part Four beautifully capture the coarseness with which the world sometimes greets love.

I thought I'd quote some passages to show you what powerful stuff you have between your hands, but there are too many—I might as well quote the whole book—and to take them out of context somehow seems offensive.

You remember how I recommended Gerasim to you, from *The Death of Ivan Ilych*. Well, in this book, we have Gerasim's equally domestic but petty antithesis: Mr. Wurtle.

Beware of Mr. Wurtle, Mr. Harper.

I can't resist quoting. On page 30:

But the surety of my love is not dismayed by any eventuality which prudence or pity can conjure up, and in the end all that we can do is to sit at the table over which our hands cross, listening to tunes from the wurlitzer, with love huge and simple between us, and nothing more to be said.

On page 44:

When the Ford rattles up to the door, five minutes (five years) late, and he walks across the lawn under the pepper-trees, I stand behind the gauze curtains, unable to move to meet him, or to speak, as I turn to liquid to invade his every orifice when he opens the door.

Grandly romantic? Yes. Highly impractical? Absolutely. But as she asks one of the police officers who arrests her, on page 55:

What do you live for then?
I don't go for that sort of thing, the officer said, I'm a family man, I belong to the Rotary Club.

She might as well have been Jesus, and the officer surely wished later that he had been more like the humble Roman centurion of Capernaum.

There is this paragraph, on page 65, after she has returned to her native Ottawa, banished there for her extraconjugal illegality:

And over the fading wooden houses I sense the reminiscences of the pioneers' passion, and the determination of early statesmen who were mild but individual and able to allude to Shakespeare while discussing politics under the elms.

I wonder if she visited Laurier House.

By Grand Central Station is a masterly—or, better, mistressly—evocation of love. A life untouched by Elizabeth Smart's kind of passion is a life not fully lived. About that, we can take her word.

Who would have thought that language could do so much? Who would have thought that grunts would so recall the miracle of the world?

Yours truly,
Yann Martel

P.S. Please thank Susan Ross, from your office, for replying to me on your behalf about the first book I sent you. Perhaps you could lend Ms. Ross your copy of Ivan Ilych *once you've finished with it?*

ELIZABETH SMART (1913–1986) was a Canadian novelist and poet. She was born into an influential family in Ottawa, and travelled extensively, working in the United States and the United Kingdom. While in London, she read a book of George Barker's poetry and fell in love, first with the writing and then with the man. Their relationship is the basis of her best-known work, *By Grand Central Station I Sat Down and Wept,* which she wrote in British Columbia. She settled in England and continued a long-term affair with the married Barker, with whom she had four children. She worked as a copywriter for thirteen years, then as an editor for *Queen* magazine, and retired to a cottage in Suffolk.

BOOK 5

THE BHAGAVAD GITA

June 11, 2007

To Stephen Harper,
Prime Minister of Canada,
This book of Hindu Wisdom,
From a Canadian writer,
With best wishes,
Yann Martel

Dear Mr. Harper,

With this fifth book, I am taking you in a direction you might find surprising: Hindu scripture. There is much Hindu scripture about, into the thousands of pages. You might have heard of the Vedas, especially the Rigveda, or of the Upanishads, or of the two great Sanskrit epics the Mahabharata and the Ramayana, among many others. In their lengthy and varied entirety, they are the sum total of the thinking about life of an ancient and still thriving civilization, that which started in the Indus Valley, the place that today we call India. It's all quite dizzying. If you feel that you know nothing, that you are paralyzed with fear and ignorance, don't worry: we all feel that way. I'm sure even devout Hindus feel that way at times.

That feeling of fear and ignorance is in fact a good starting place, because it's exactly how Arjuna feels at the beginning of the *Bhagavad Gita*, the book you now have in your hands. The *Gita* is one short part of the Mahabharata, a much longer text, and it is the best known of Hindu scriptures, certainly the most widely read, and because of that arguably the most important. What Arjuna needs, what I need, what you need, what we all need, is a lesson in dharma, in proper conduct. And that is the lesson that Arjuna receives from Krishna, who is Arjuna's charioteer and friend but who also happens to be the Lord Supreme God of All Things.

Arjuna is on the eve of a great battle. He has asked Krishna to drive their chariot between the two facing armies and he surveys the assembled mass of soldiers. He sees that he has friends and enemies on both sides and he knows that many will die. That is when he loses heart.

Arjuna's battle may have its origins in a real, historical event, but in the *Bhagavad Gita* we are to read it as a metaphor. The true battle here is the battle of life and each one of us is an Arjuna facing his or her life, with all its daunting challenges.

I suggest you read neither the introduction by the scholar nor that by the translator, though Juan Mascaró's translation is excellent; that's why I chose it for you. It's clear and poetic, uncluttered by jargon or pedantry. Read it aloud and you will feel the cosmic wind blowing through the words. But the introductions, leave aside, I suggest, because it is the same thing with Hinduism as with every religion: there are matters of history and there are matters of faith. The Jesus of history is one thing, the Jesus of faith another. Search too far into the Jesus of history and you will lose yourself in anthropology and miss the point. The *Gita* of faith—much like the Jesus of faith—will have its greatest influence on you if you take it entirely on its own terms, making your own way through its grand injunctions and baffling mysteries. The *Gita* is a dialogue between one man and God, and the best reading of it, at least initially, is as a dialogue between one reader and the text. After that first encounter, if you want, scholars can be of help.

There may be ideas here that will irk you. By Western standards, there is a streak of fatalism running through Hinduism that will bother some. We live in a highly individualistic culture and we make much of the exertions of our egos. Perhaps if we took to heart one of the fundamental lessons of the *Gita*—to take action with detachment—we might exert ourselves in a calmer way and see that the ego, in the scheme of things, really is a puny, transitory thing.

Read the *Bhagavad Gita* in a moment of stillness and with an open heart, and it will change you. It is a majestic text, elevated and elevating. Like Arjuna, you will emerge from this dialogue with Krishna wiser and more serene, ready for action but filled with inner peace and loving-kindness.

Om shanti (peace be with you), as they say in India.

Yours truly,
Yann Martel

BOOK 6

BONJOUR TRISTESSE
BY FRANÇOISE SAGAN

June 25, 2007

To Stephen Harper,
Prime Minister of Canada,
From a Canadian writer,
With best wishes,
Yann Martel

Dear Mr. Harper,

From London, England, I'm sending you an English translation of a French novel. In this novel people smoke, people get slapped in the face, people drink heavily and then drive home, people have nothing but the blackest coffee for breakfast, and always people are concerned with love. Very French *d'une certaine époque.*

Bonjour Tristesse came out in France in 1954. Its author, Françoise Sagan, was nineteen years old. Immediately she became a celebrity and her book a bestseller.

More than that: they both became symbols.

Bonjour Tristesse is narrated in the first person by seventeen-year-old Cécile. She describes her father, Raymond, as "a frivolous man, clever at business, always curious, quickly bored, and attractive to women." The business cleverness is never mentioned again, but clearly it has allowed Raymond to enjoy freely his other attributes, his frivolity, curiosity, boredom and attraction, all of which revolve around dalliances of the heart and loins. He and his beloved daughter share the same temperament and they are in the south of France for the summer holidays with Elsa, his latest young mistress. This triangle suites Cécile perfectly and she is assiduous at pursuing her idle seaside pleasures, which come to include Cyril, a handsome young man who is keen on her.

But all is ruined when her father invites Anne to stay with them. She's an old friend of the family, a handsome woman her father's age, made of sterner, more sober stuff. She starts to meddle in Cécile's life. Worse, a few weeks after arriving, fun Elsa is dumped when Raymond starts a relationship with Anne. And finally, not long after, Anne announces that she and her father are planning to get married. Cécile is aghast. Her serial frolicker of a father and Anne, husband and wife? She, Cécile, a stepdaughter to Anne, who will work hard to transform her into a serious and studious young person? *Quel cauchemar!* Cécile sets to work to thwart things, using Elsa and Cyril as her pawns. The results are tragic.

After the grim work of the Second World War and the hard work of the post-war reconstruction, *Bonjour Tristesse* burst onto the French literary scene like a carnival. It announced what seemed like a new species, youth, *la jeunesse,* who had but one message: have fun with us or be gone; stay up all night at a jazz club or never come out with us again; don't talk to us about marriage and other boring conventions; let's smoke and be idle instead; forget the future—who's the new lover? As for the *tristesse* of the title, it was an excuse for a really good pout.

Such a brash, proudly indolent attitude, coming with an open contempt for conventional values, landed like a bomb among the bourgeoisie. Françoise Sagan earned herself a papal denunciation, which she must have relished.

A book can do that, capture a time and a spirit, be the

expression of a broad yearning running through society. Read the book and you will understand not only the characters but the Zeitgeist. Sometimes the book will be one a group strongly identifies with—for example, *On the Road*, by Jack Kerouac, among American youth—or, conversely, strongly identifies against— Salman Rushdie's *The Satanic Verses* among some Muslims.

So that too is what a book can be, a thermometer revealing a fever.

Yours truly,
Yann Martel

FRANÇOISE SAGAN (1935–2004), born Françoise Quoirez, was a novelist, playwright and screenwriter. Sagan's novels centre around disillusioned bourgeois characters (often teenagers) and primarily romantic themes; her work has been compared to that of J.D. Salinger. The writer François Mauriac described her as "a charming little monster." Her oeuvre includes dozens of works for print and performance. She suffered a car accident in 1957, an experience that left her addicted to painkillers and other drugs for much of her life.

BOOK 7

CANDIDE
BY VOLTAIRE
July 9, 2007

To Stephen Harper,
Prime Minister of Canada,
This witty book on evil,
From a Canadian writer,
With best wishes,
Yann Martel

Dear Mr. Harper,

You've no doubt heard the theory of six degrees of separation, how each one of us on this planet is connected to everyone else through a chain of five people. Well, in a way, you and I are linked through the seventh book I am sending you, *Candide*, by Voltaire. Let me explain. On pages 110 and 111 of Chapter XXIII there is a brief scene in which Candide, having just arrived in Portsmouth, England, witnesses the execution of a British admiral. "Why execute this admiral?" asks Candide.

"Because he had not enough dead men to his credit," comes the reply.

This incident was no invention of Voltaire's. There was indeed a British admiral who was executed for failing to "do his utmost" during a naval battle with the French off the island of Minorca. He was the first and only British admiral so treated by Britannia, and his name was John Byng.

Do you recognize that last name? That's right: Lord Byng

of Vimy, of the "King-Byng Affair," Governor General of Canada from 1921 to 1926, and a direct descendant of the ill-fated Admiral Byng. I'm sure you have regular meetings with Lord Byng's current successor, Her Excellency Michaëlle Jean. And the last degree of separation: a direct descendant of both Byngs, Jamie Byng, is a good friend of mine and my British publisher. So there you have it, six degrees of separation: me-Voltaire-Byng-Byng-Byng-Jean-you.

It's in this same Chapter XXIII of *Candide,* in the paragraph just before Admiral Byng's execution in fact, that Voltaire famously dismissed Canada as "a few acres of snow," "quelques arpents de neige." Isn't that amazing? Voltaire speaks of Canada and then right after tells a story about a mutual acquaintance of ours. Mr. Harper, the link between us couldn't be more preordained than that!

One last anecdote. I can also say this of *Candide:* not once but twice I have come upon people reading a book, thought I recognized the title, exclaimed what a great novel it was, anticipating some good talk about the terrible, funny calamities that poor Candide must endure, only to be told by the readers, in both cases women, that the "e" was an "a" and that the book they were reading was not Voltaire's brilliant satire but rather a book on candida, which is a bothersome, often recurring and terribly itchy yeast infection of the vagina. After that, as you can imagine, the conversation became a bit stilted.

Let's get to the point. *Candide,* published in 1759, is a short, funny and engaging tale about a serious problem: evil and the suffering it engenders. Voltaire lived between 1694 and 1778 and was one of the great gadflies of his time. In *Candide* he lampooned what he felt was the facile optimism of the day, an optimism best expressed by the philosopher Gottfried Leibniz's formulation that our world is "the best of all possible worlds" (you might remember that line from an ironic Kris Kristofferson song). The reasoning behind this conclusion was that since God is good and all-powerful, the world cannot be anything but the best conceivable world, with the optimum combination of elements. Evil was thus posited as serving the purpose of maximizing good, since it is in having a choice between good and evil that we fallible human beings can improve ourselves and become good.

Now, we can perhaps agree that adversity can bring the best out of us, and it is still Christian doctrine that we are "perfected by suffering." But such a blithe justification of evil has fairly obvious limits. It might do for the sort of evil that comes as a kick-in-the-behind, as a retrospective blessing in disguise. But will it serve for heinous evil and egregious misfortune?

Voltaire wrote *Candide* in part as a reaction to just such an instance of misfortune. On the morning of November 1, 1755, a cataclysmic earthquake struck Lisbon. Immediately, most churches in the city collapsed, killing thousands of people who were inside. Other public buildings also came down, as did over 12,000 dwellings. Once the tremors had stopped, a tsunami struck the city, and after that, fires wreaked further havoc. Over sixty thousand people were killed and the material damage, in an age still innocent of the destructive power of modern bombs, was unprecedented. The Lisbon earthquake had the same troubling effect on people at the time as the Holocaust had in our time. But whereas the Nazi barbarity had us mostly wondering about human nature, the Lisbon earthquake had people wondering about the nature of God. How could God allow such cruelty to take place in a city as piously Catholic and evangelical as Lisbon, and of all days on All Saints' Day? In what conceivable way could killing so many people in one stroke maximize the good of this world?

Answering such troubling questions—the Holy Grail of theodicy—remains as troubling then as now. Perhaps the answer still is that we lack perspective, that in a way that we mortals just can't understand, great evil is part of a divine plan and makes ultimate sense.

In the meantime, until God comes down and fully explains that plan, evil galls. Voltaire was religiously outraged by the Lisbon earthquake. For him it was clear: there was no Providence, there was no God. To be eternally optimistic in the face of great evil and suffering was not only insensitive to its victims, but morally and intellectually untenable. He set to prove it in the story of Candide, the naive young man from Thunder-ten-tronckh, in Westphalia, who could have had as his motto "All is for the best," such an optimist was he at the start of the novel. Wait till you see all the catastrophes that befall him. The novel ends, when all has been said and done and suffered, with a simple call to quiet, peaceable and collective work: "we must go and work in the garden," "il faut cultiver notre jardin."

That call still stands as perhaps the only practical solution to what we can do in the face of evil: spend our time simply, fruitfully and with others.

Yours truly,
Yann Martel

VOLTAIRE (1694–1778), born François-Marie Arouet, was a French Enlightenment writer and philosopher. He was immensely prolific, writing novels, poetry, plays, essays, scientific papers and historical works. Voltaire was politically active, supporting social reform, free trade, civil liberties and freedom of religion. He was a fierce critic of the Catholic Church. His satire got him into trouble: in 1717, he was imprisoned for eleven months in the Bastille for criticizing the French government; and in 1726 he was exiled from France for three years for insulting a member of the aristocracy. He is buried in the Pantheon in Paris.

BOOK 8

SHORT AND SWEET:
101 VERY SHORT POEMS
EDITED BY SIMON ARMITAGE

July 23, 2007

To Stephen Harper,
Prime Minister of Canada,
A book of concise loveliness,
From a Canadian writer,
With best wishes,
Yann Martel

Dear Mr. Harper,

You said a few years ago that your favourite book was the *Guinness Book of World Records.* Well, as a dedicated reader of those yearly volumes that means that at least on one occasion you read a poem. Simon Armitage, the editor of *Short and Sweet: 101 Very Short Poems,* the latest book I am sending you, says in his introduction that he became interested in very short poetry as a teenager when he read in the aforementioned *Guinness* book what was claimed to be the world's shortest poem:

Fleas

Adam
'ad 'em

A masterpiece, isn't it? In a single rhyming couplet of four syllables something is suggested about the ancient and intimate relations between humans and animals, about the great antiquity of small, neglected beings, about the shabby reality of our existence, divine origins notwithstanding, and the corruption of this world, inherent even in the Garden of Eden. And there's more: in that rhyme that sounds like "Adam, Adam," is there not a lament? Or is it an accusation? Either way, it could be that the fleas in question are us.

You can't beat poetry for saying so much with so little.

Busy? Tired? Feeling nothing? You're missing on the depth of life that you know is out there but you don't have time to read a big fat novel? Then try this poem, by George Mackay Brown:

Taxman

Seven scythes leaned at the wall.
Beard upon golden beard
The last barley load
Swayed through the yard.
The girls uncorked the ale.
Fiddle and feet moved together.
Then between stubble and heather
A horseman rode.

Notice the extraordinary concision with which a narrative structure is set up, with the emotional questions and possibilities left to ripple through the reader's mind. The marvel of poetry is that it can be as short as a question yet as powerful as an answer. For example, the following poem, by Stephen Crane:

In the Desert

In the desert
I saw a creature, naked, bestial
Who, squatting upon de ground
Held his heart in his hands
And ate of it. I said, "Is it good, friend?"
"It is bitter–bitter," he answered:
"But I like it
Because it is bitter,
And because it is my heart."

I envy that of poets, that ability to create something so small that nevertheless feels so complete, the vastness of existence made to fit into something no bigger than a coin purse. Look at this poem, by Hugo Williams:

Lights Out

We're allowed to talk for ten minutes
about what has happened during the day,
then we have to go to sleep.
It doesn't matter what we dream about.

Repetition suits poetry. Read one of these poems several times and you'll see for yourself: it keeps getting better. In this case, familiarity breeds respect.

A last one, lovely, by Wendy Cope:

Flowers

Some men never think of it.
You did. You'd come along
And say you'd nearly brought me flowers
But something had gone wrong. The shop was
          closed. Or you had doubts—
The sort that minds like ours
Dream up instantly. You thought
I might not want your flowers.
It made me smile and hug you then.
Now I can only smile.
But, look, the flowers you nearly brought
Have lasted all this while.

Short though they are, I wouldn't rush through any of these poems. Rush tends to disturb their echoing stillness. Best to read them aloud, getting the rhythm right, smoothing out the stumbles, slowly getting a sense of their sense.

It's a marvellous exercise in—in what?—in being human, I suppose.

Yours truly,
Yann Martel

SIMON ARMITAGE (b. 1963) is a British poet, novelist and playwright known for his dry wit and accessible style. He is the author of nine books of poetry, and has written and presented works for radio and television. He has earned multiple awards for his poetry, including the *Sunday Times* Author of the Year Award, a Forward Poetry Prize, a Lannan Award, an Ivor Novello Award and the title of the

UK's Millennium Poet for his poem "Killing Time." Armitage has been a judge for the Griffin Poetry Prize and the Man Booker Prize for Fiction.

BOOK 9

CHRONICLE OF A DEATH FORETOLD
BY GABRIEL GARCÍA MÁRQUEZ

August 6, 2007

To Stephen Harper,
Prime Minister of Canada,
From a Canadian writer,
With best wishes,
Yann Martel

Dear Mr. Harper,

When I found a used copy of the latest book that I'm sending you, I was pleased that it was a hard cover—a first after eight paperbacks—but I was disappointed with the cover artwork.* Surely, *Chronicle of a Death Foretold*, the short novel by the great Gabriel García Márquez, deserves better than this awkward job. Who chose the purple? It's all so hideous. But you can't judge a book by its cover, isn't that right?

Which is a nice way of broaching the topic of clichés.

A cliché, to remind you, is a worn, hackneyed phrase or opinion. At one time, perhaps in the Middle Ages among monks slowly copying books by hand in a monastery, the notion that nothing of substance can be judged by its surface, expressed in terms of a bound stack of paper and its protective shell, must

---

* The cover features an unappealing drawing of a bride. She looks like a stiff porcelain doll.

have seemed like a dazzling revelation that had the monks looking at each other in amazement and rushing out to sing in full-throated worship to *urbi et orbi:* "Praise be to God! A book can't be judged by its cover! Hallelujah, hallelujah!"

But now, even among people who don't read a book a year, it's a cliché, it's a lazy, thoughtless way of expressing oneself.

Sometimes clichés are unavoidable. "I love you"—a sentence that is foundational to the well-being of every human being, the "you" being another person, a group of people, a grand notion or cause, a god, or simply a reflection in the mirror—is a cliché. Every actor who has to say the line struggles to deliver it in a way that makes it sound fresh, like Adam saying it for the first time to Eve. But there's no good way of saying it otherwise—and no one really tries to. We live very well with "I love you" because the syntactical simplicity of it—one each of subject, verb, object, nothing else—nicely matches its intended truthfulness. So we happily blurt out the cliché, some of us repeating it several times, for emphasis, or some of us saying it all the time, for example at the end of every phone call with a family member. Lovers at a balcony, sons and daughters at war, dervishes whirling—they're all living "I love you" in a way that is not clichéd but essential.

But otherwise clichés should be avoided like the West Nile virus. Why? Because they are stale and flat, and because they are contagious. Convenient writerly shortcuts, hurried means of signifying "you know what I mean," clichés at first are just a froth of tiny white eggs in the ink of your pen, incubated slowly by the warmth of your lazy fingers. The harm to your prose is slight, and people are forgiving. But convenience, shortcuts and hurry are no way to write true words, and if you are not careful—and it is hard work to be careful—the eggs multiply, bloom and enter your blood.

The damage can be serious. The infection can spread to your eyes, to your nose, to your tongue, to your ears, to your skin, and worse: to your brain and to your heart. It's no longer just your words, written and spoken, that are conventional, conformist, unoriginal, dull. Now it's your very thoughts and feelings that have lost their heartbeat. In the most serious cases, the person can no longer even see or feel the world directly, but can only perceive it through the reductive, muffling filter of cliché.

At this stage, the cliché attains its political dimension: dogmatism. Dogmatism in politics has exactly the same effect as the cliché in writing: it prevents the soul from interacting openly and honestly with the world, with that pragmatism that lets in fresh all the beautiful, bountiful messiness of life.

The cliché and dogmatism—two related banes that all writers and politicians should avoid if we are to serve well our respective constituencies.

As for the García Márquez book, I got it for you because of your recent trip to—and renewed interest in—Latin America. The man's a genius.

Yours truly,
Yann Martel

GABRIEL GARCÍA MÁRQUEZ (b. 1927) is an internationally acclaimed novelist, short story writer, screenplay writer, memoirist and journalist. During his long literary career, he has been credited with popularizing the "magical realism" writing style. Márquez, nicknamed "Gabo," sets his stories in Latin America and often addresses the themes of isolation, love and memory. His bestknown works are *One Hundred Years of Solitude* and *Love in the Time of Cholera*. He is also well known for his political activism. He received the Nobel Prize in Literature in 1982. Raised in Colombia, he now lives in Mexico City.

BOOK 10

MISS JULIA
BY AUGUST STRINDBERG

August 20, 2007

To Stephen Harper,
Prime Minister of Canada,
From a Canadian writer,
With best wishes,
Yann Martel

Dear Mr. Harper,

One day when August Strindberg was still a student at the University of Uppsala, he received a surprising summons: King Karl XV wanted to see him. Strindberg put on his best suit and made the short trip to the Royal Palace in Stockholm. The twenty-two-year-old was from an undistinguished family, he was very poor, and his academic achievements were perfectly average, but the King of Sweden had his reasons for wanting to meet him: he was keen on the arts and he had seen a performance of a historical play that Strindberg had written, *The Outlaw,* and he had liked it. In fact, he had liked it so much that he promised the young man a quarterly stipend so that he could finish his university studies. Strindberg was delighted. Alas, after only two payments and without any explanation, the royal bounty dried up. So it goes. Strindberg dropped out of university.

By all accounts, Strindberg was a miserable sod. He had a boundless capacity to be unhappy, especially in his relations with women. But he also had a mind of immense energy, intelligence and originality, and he wrote brilliant plays.

A brilliant play is something very peculiar. Drama is the most oral of literary forms, far less of an artifice than the short story, the novel or the poem, and far less reliant on publication to fully come into its own; what really counts for a play is not that it be read, but that it be seen, in the flesh. In many ways, life has all the trappings of a play: when you, Mr. Harper, enter the House of Commons, for example, you are walking onto a stage. And you are there because you are playing a role, the lead role. And it is because you are playing that role that you rise and speak. And then in Hansard the next day it reads like a play. It is the same for all of us in life: we move about on various stages, we take on various roles, and we speak. But there is a crucial difference, of course, one that goes to the core of what art is: in a play there is structure and meaning, put there by the playwright, while in life, even after many acts, the structure and meaning is hard to find. Some claim to know of a great playwright who has authored our existence, but even for them structure and meaning remains an ongoing challenge.

So while a play approximates life to a great degree, it is in other ways nothing like life. No one speaks with the concise completeness of the dramatis personae of a play, neither in ways that so quickly yet subtly reveal their character, nor with a tempo that so rises and falls until a climax, nor, usually, in a space so confined as a stage's. In a phrase: life is a play that doesn't make sense, while a play is life that does.

(Admittedly, there are people for whom life makes perfect sense, their vision of things forever untouched by doubt, the entropy of time seeming to have no more effect on them than a gentle breeze on the face. They are the type who will not go for the questioning of life that is a play, indeed, that is all great art. But that is a separate matter.)

The knack for writing plays is a knack I don't have. I have tried to move plot entirely through dialogue, I have tried to express my thoughts on life within the strictures of speech, I have tried to develop an ear for the way people speak—to laughable, unpublishable result. Notice how the word is play*wright;* it may sound like *write,* but originally the act of writing a play struck the English as more akin to the work of a carpenter than of a writer. The world of letters is indeed easily divided between those who *write* and those who *wright.* There are exceptions—Samuel Beckett, for example—but those who can do both successfully are not many.

There are three plays in the volume of Strindberg that I have sent you. It is the middle play, known either as *Miss Julia* or *Miss Julie,* that I recommend to you. In it you will read dialogue that is so brilliant, so crackling with tension, so straightforward on the surface yet hinting at such turmoil and complexity, that it will, paradoxically, all seem perfectly natural to you. That is the sign of a great play in the naturalist tradition: how easily it flows. One gets the sense that the playwright just sat down with a good, simple idea and it all came out in an easy afternoon's work. I assure you that that is like thinking that all Michelangelo had to do was chip away from the block of marble everything that didn't look like David.

Miss Julia, which was first performed in 1889, is about confinement, principally the confinement of sexual roles and the confinement of class. Miss Julia and Jean, her servant, meet, match and clash, with tragic consequences. I would love to see the play actually performed on a stage. The alchemy of great play, great director and great actors is rare, but when it happens—I am remembering now a performance long ago at Stratford of Eugene

O'Neill's *Long Day's Journey into Night,* with Hume Cronyn and Jessica Tandy—it makes for an experience of an intensity that is, in my estimation, unmatched in the literary arts.

You will notice that the previous owner of your copy of Strindberg wrote copiously in the margins. This annoyed me at first, this defacing of *Miss Julia.* But finally I was charmed by the intruder's thoughts and opinions. The handwriting is large, clear and loopy; I think it is a young person writing, likely a young woman. Above Jean's comment that "on the way back by the barn I looked in and joined the dancing," our hypothetical young woman writes "*joie de vivre.*" When Jean impudently tells Miss Julia that he knows that Kristin, the cook, talks in her sleep because "I've heard her," our young woman observes "Kristin's his mistress." She variously thinks Jean to be "practical" or "realistic," while Miss Julia is "totally impractical." Other short notations of hers are "dramatic moment," "flirting," "bourgeoisie," "gives her warning," "seduction" and "trag. everyth falling apart" (sic).

One last thing, to elucidate a point easily missed: the "Turkish pavilion" on page 90 that Jean mentions sneaking into as a child, the "finest building I'd ever seen," the walls "covered with pictures of kings and emperors," his first time "inside a castle," is just a fancy outhouse—and the way out he is forced to take when he hears someone approaching is the exit you'd least like to take if you were in an outhouse.

Yours truly,
Yann Martel

AUGUST STRINDBERG (1849–1912) is best known for his plays, but he also wrote short stories, novels, poems and volumes of autobiography.

In addition to his writing, he was a painter and photographer, and experimented with alchemy. In life and in his art, he was pessimistic and his works were marked by his overt satirizing of Swedish society. Strindberg's plays fall into two categories—naturalistic and expressionistic—and he is considered one of the pioneers of Expressionism. He wrote dozens of plays, the most famous of which are the naturalistic *Miss Julia* and *The Father*.

BOOK II

THE WATSONS
BY JANE AUSTEN
September 3, 2007

To Stephen Harper,
Prime Minister of Canada,
From a Canadian writer,
With best wishes,
Yann Martel

Dear Mr. Harper,

The great Jane Austen. She is a shining example of how art—
like politics—can take the least promising ore and transform it
into the finest metal. Austen had three things going against her:
she lived in *rural* England, she was middle class in the age before
that class exploded with possibilities, and she was a woman. That
is to say, her life was hemmed in by limitations.

England during Austen's lifetime—1775 to 1817—was in the
full throes of the Industrial Revolution, and revolutions are
occasions of great upheaval and renewal, both for the arts and
for politics. But Austen mostly missed out on this revolution
because she lived outside of the urban centres that were at its
heart. And in the genteel hinterland where she lived, she was a
member of a most precarious class: the landless *middle* class,
with a class she wished not to join swimming beneath her, the
working class, and a class she wished she could join soaring
above, the nobility. This precariousness was aggravated by her
being a woman, which disqualified her from whatever work a

member of the middle class might decently do: the clergy, the medical profession, the military. So all Austen's female characters worry endlessly about financial security, yet have only a single way of achieving it: marriage. Hungry for status and material goods, but unwilling (because unable) to earn them, always on the hunt for wealthy husbands, yet having only stuffiness, rigidity and pretence to offer—I suspect that if we met the female members of Jane Austen's class today, with our modern sensibilities, we would find them deeply disagreeable. There is this exchange between two female characters in *The Watsons*, the latest book I am sending you:

"To be so bent on marriage, to pursue a man merely for the sake of situation is a sort of thing that shocks me; I cannot understand it. Poverty is a great evil, but to a woman of education and feeling it ought not, it cannot be the greatest. I would rather be teacher at a school (and I can think of nothing worse) than marry a man I did not like."

"I would rather do anything than be teacher at a school," said her sister. "*I* have been at school, Emma, and know what a life they lead; *you* never have. I should not like marrying a disagreeable man any more than yourself, but I do not think there *are* many very disagreeable men; I think I could like any good-humoured man with a comfortable income."

How sad to have the most important profession in the world thought of as worse than what has facetiously been called the oldest profession in the world. Thankfully, things have changed. Today, the middle class in Canada has expanded to absorb all other classes, so that practically everyone is of the working class, the class that works, and the sinking and the soaring is called mobility, and it is a triumph of our time that women can avail themselves of that mobility (though still not as much as men—there's still some liberating work that needs doing).

But back to Jane Austen: boxed in, left only to play card games, look forward to the next ball and keep an eye out for eligible bachelors, surrounded by green pastures and rolling hills, does this strike you as promising grounds for great art?

Well, in the case of Jane Austen, it was. Because she had the great and good luck of having a loving and intellectually lively family, and she was blessed with a keen and critical sense of observation, as well as an inherently positive disposition.

So though limited by class and by sex, Jane Austen was able to transcend these limitations. Her novels are marvels of wit and perspicacity, and in them she examined her society with such fresh and engaging realism that the English novel was durably changed.

The Watsons is easily Jane Austen's least-known work. But I selected it for you for two reasons: it is short, and it is unfinished. Its shortness will I hope make you want to read some of Austen's longer novels, *Pride and Prejudice* or *Emma* perhaps.

And though it is unfinished, an abandoned draft, there is more perfection in it than in many a completed novel. Austen abandoned *The Watsons* in 1805 as a result of personal difficulties: the death of a good friend, and right afterwards the illness and death of her own father, which left her and her sister and her mother in uncertain circumstances. Eventually, four years later, her brother Edward was able to provide his mother and sisters with a cottage, and Austen began writing again.

She let go and then started up again, able to produce novels that marked the English novel forever. In that, there is something instructive. There is so much we must leave unfinished. How hard it is to let go.

Yours truly,
Yann Martel

JANE AUSTEN (1775–1817) was an English novelist whose realist works offer strong female characters and biting social commentary. She never married, and lived with her family until her death at the age of forty-one. Several of her novels have been adapted for the screen. Her novels are still popular today, and *Pride and Prejudice* has inspired modern spoofs including *Bridget Jones's Diary* by Helen Fielding, the Bollywood film *Bride & Prejudice* directed by Gurinder Chadha, and *Pride and Prejudice and Zombies,* adapted from Austen's original novel by Seth Grahame-Smith.

BOOK 12

MAUS
BY ART SPIEGELMAN
September 17, 2007

To Stephen Harper,
Prime Minister of Canada,
This most disturbing and necessary book,
From a Canadian writer,
With best wishes,
Yann Martel

Dear Mr. Harper,

I am sorry but you will have to endure this time a letter written in my terrible handwriting. I didn't manage to find a printer in Oświęcim, the small Polish town where I'm staying at the moment.

Oświęcim is better known by the name the Germans gave it: Auschwitz. Have you been?

I am here trying to finish my next book. And it also explains my choice of the latest book I am sending you: the graphic novel *Maus,* by Art Spiegelman Don't be fooled by the format. This comic book is *real* literature.

Some stories need to be told in many different ways so that they will exist in new ways for new generations. The story of the murder of nearly six million of Europe's Jewish people at the hands of the Nazis and their criminal accomplices is just the sort of story that needs renewing if we don't want a part of ourselves to fall asleep, like grandchildren nodding off after hearing grandfather repeat the same story of yore one time too many.

I know I said I would send you books that would increase your "stillness." But a sense of peace and calm focus, of what Buddhists call "passionate detachment," must not fall into self-satisfaction or complacency. So a disturbance—and Auschwitz is profoundly disturbing—can be the right way to renew one's stillness.

Maus is a masterpiece. Spiegelman tells his story, or, more accurately, the story of his father and mother, in a bold and radical way. It's not just that he takes the graphic form, thought perhaps by some to be a medium only for children, to new artistic heights by taking on such a momentous topic as exterminationist genocide. It's more than that. It's how he tells the story. You will see. The narrative agility and ease of it. And how the frames speak large. Some, small though they are, and in black and white, have an impact that one would think possible only with large paintings or shots from a movie.

And I haven't even mentioned the main device, which explains the title of the book: all the characters have the heads of one kind of animal or other. So the Jews have the heads of mice, the Germans of cats, the Poles of pigs, the Americans of dogs, and so on.

It's brilliant. It so takes you in, it so rips you apart. From there you must make your own tricky way back again to what it means to be human.

Yours truly,
Yann Martel

ART SPIEGELMAN (b. 1948) is a Swedish-born American comic artist who was part of the underground comics movements of the 1960s and '70s, contributing to several publications and co-founding *Arcade* and *Raw*. He was a co-creator of garbage candy and Garbage Pail Kids trading cards. Named one of *TIME* magazine's "Top 100 Most Influential People" in 2005, he has won multiple awards for his work, including the Pulitzer Prize in 1992 for *Maus* and its sequel, *Maus II*. He continues to publish new work and promote the comic medium, and in 2004 published a large board book, *In the Shadow of No Towers*, about the September 11, 2001, terrorist attacks on New York City.

BOOK 13

TO KILL A MOCKINGBIRD
BY HARPER LEE
October 1, 2007

To Stephen Harper,
Prime Minister of Canada,
From a Canadian writer,
With best wishes,
Yann Martel

Dear Mr. Harper,

In an interview some years ago Mavis Gallant mentioned an operation she underwent. She awoke from general anaesthesia in a state of mental confusion. For several minutes she couldn't remember any details of her identity or of her life, not her name or her age or what she did, not where she was nor why she was there. An amnesia that was complete—except for this: she knew she was a woman and that she was thinking in English. Inextricably linked to the faintest glimmer of consciousness were those two identity traits: sex and language.

Which says how deep language goes. It becomes part of our biology. Our lungs need and are made for air, our mouths and stomachs need and are made for nutrition; our ears and noses can hear and smell and, lo, there are things to be heard and smelled. The mind is the same: it needs and is made for language, and, lo, there are things to be said and understood.

I am no champion of any particular language. Every language, from Afrikaans to Zulu, does the job it is required to do: map the world with sounds that conveniently identify objects and concepts. Given a little time, every living language spoken by a sufficient number of people will match any new object or concept with a new word. Have you heard the notion of how the Inuit are supposed to have twenty-six words for snow, while we in English have only the one, "snow"? Well, that's nonsense. Ask avid English-language skiers and they'll come up with twenty-six words or compounds to describe snow.

Just as there are many cuisines on this earth, many styles of dress and many understandings of the divine, each of which can keep the stomach content, the body smartly covered and the soul attuned to the eternal, so there are many different kinds of sounds with which we can make ourselves understood. Each language has its own sonority, cadence, specialized vocabulary, and so on, but it all evens out. Each of us can be fully human in any language.

But since you are a native English speaker, let me champion English in this letter as an introduction to the latest semi-monthly book I am sending you. The English language has by far the largest vocabulary of any language on earth, well over 600,000 words. French, by comparison, is said to have 350,000 words and Italian, 250,000. Now right away, before I get jumped upon by those from my native province and all my Italian-speaking friends, this exuberance of vocabulary is largely irrelevant. Just 7,000 words represent 90 percent of the root vocabulary the average English speaker uses.

And let's not forget: the voluble Italians showed no reticence in launching—and thoroughly enjoying—their *Renascimento* with their fewer words while the reserved Britons sat in their dark and dank island idling away the hours of pouring rain by wondering whether they should adopt the Italian word for that explosion of optimism and sunshine or call it the *Rebirth* or the *Renaissance.*

How did a local-yokel language spoken on an island—truly, an insular language—come to span the globe? The explanation can be summarized in two words: *invasions* and counter-invasions; that is, *colonialism*. The Germanic language of the Anglo-Saxons was immeasurably enriched by a number of invasions. In linguistic terms, the Christianization of Britannia was a beachhead, the Norman invasion of 1066 was a flood, and the Renaissance was a flourish. After that, the verbally empowered English set out to conquer the world, a great plundering that made them wealthy, not only with other people's gold but also with other people's words.

English is a hot stew of many ingredients. In it can be found words that have their origin in Arabic, Breton, Czech, Danish, Finnish, Gaelic, Hindi, Inuit, Japanese, Latin, Malay, Norwegian, Polish, Russian, Spanish, Turkish, Welsh, to mention only a selection. And that's only vocabulary. English usage—how people speak their English—is also extraordinarily varied.

And that's the reason for my gift to you this time: *To Kill a Mockingbird,* by Harper Lee. It's a modern classic, a great story, one that will make you love lawyers, but it's for the usage that I chose it. Rural Alabama English of the 1950s as spoken by children is something else. And yet it is English, so you will understand it without a problem. That is the rare privilege of those who speak English: in reading untranslated books from every continent they can feel both at home and abroad.

Bonne lecture!

Yours truly,
Yann Martel

HARPER LEE (b. 1926) is an American writer, best-known for her Pulitzer Prize–winning novel *To Kill a Mockingbird.* This novel, which is frequently taught in schools to this day, was made into an Academy Award–winning film starring Gregory Peck as Atticus Finch. Many autobiographical elements are present in the novel, and the character of Dill is based on Lee's lifelong friend Truman Capote. After publishing her book to instant acclaim and long-lasting success, Lee retreated from public life. To date, *To Kill a Mockingbird* is the only work she has published beyond the scope of magazines.

BOOK 14:

LE PETIT PRINCE
BY ANTOINE DE SAINT-EXUPÉRY

October 15, 2007

To Stephen Harper,
Prime Minister of Canada,
Ce livre en français,
From a Canadian writer,
With best wishes,
Yann Martel

Cher Monsieur Harper,

Vous parlez le français. Vous avez fait de grands et fructueux efforts pour apprendre et parler cette langue depuis que vous êtes premier ministre. Vous espérez ainsi apprivoiser les Québécois.

Par ailleurs, la dernière fois, je vous ai beaucoup entretenu de l'anglais. Alors cette fois-ci je vous envoie un livre en français. Il est très connu. C'est *Le Petit Prince*, de l'écrivain français Antoine de Saint-Exupéry. Vous l'avez peut-être lu au cours de vos études mais il saura vous être encore assurément très utile, non seulement pour maintenir votre français, mais aussi pour vous aider auprès des Québécois, puisque *Le Petit Prince* c'est aussi l'histoire d'un apprivoisement, dans ce cas-ci, d'un renard.

Le renard fait cadeau d'une très importante leçon au Petit Prince, mais je ne vais pas la répéter. Je vous laisse la redécouvrir.

Le vocabulaire est simple, les scènes claires à comprendre, la morale évidente et attachante. C'est en fait un conte chrétien.

Vous allez soupirer, "Si seulement les Québécois étaient aussi faciles à apprivoiser que les renards."

Mais nous sommes plutôt, nous Québécois, comme la fleur du Petit Prince, avec notre orgueil et nos quatre épines.

Cordialement vôtre,
Yann Martel

[TRANSLATION]

Dear Mr. Harper,

You speak French. You've made great and fruitful efforts to learn the language since you became Prime Minister. You hope in this way to tame Quebeckers.

In my last letter, I discussed the English language. So this time I'm sending you a book in French, one that is very well known. It's *The Little Prince*, by the French writer Antoine de Saint-Exupéry. You perhaps read it during your French-language studies, but I'm certain it will still be of use to you, not only to help you maintain your French, but also to help you with Quebeckers, since *The Little Prince* is also the story of a taming, in this case of a fox.

The fox teaches the Little Prince a very important life lesson, but I won't divulge it here. I'll leave it for you to find it.

The vocabulary is simple, the scenes easy to understand, the moral obvious and endearing. It's a Christian tale.

You'll sigh, "If only Quebeckers were so easy to tame."

But we Quebeckers are rather like the Little Prince's flower, with our pride and our four thorns.

Yours truly,
Yann Martel

ANTOINE DE SAINT-EXUPÉRY (1900–1944), a French novelist and artist, is most famous for his illustrated philosophical novella, *Le Petit Prince* (*The Little Prince*). This story is so beloved that Saint-Exupéry's drawing of the Little Prince was printed on the French 50-franc note until the introduction of the euro. Saint-Exupéry was an aviator and, in most of his works, including *Night Flight* and *Wind, Sand and Stars*, he drew on his experiences as a pilot. He worked as a pilot for the postal service for years. During World War II, he flew reconnaissance missions for the Allies. On one of these flights he went missing and was presumed dead.

BOOK 15

ORANGES ARE NOT THE ONLY FRUIT
BY JEANETTE WINTERSON

October 29, 2007

To Stephen Harper,
From an English writer,
With best wishes,
Jeanette Winterson
(sent to you by a Canadian writer, Yann Martel)

Dear Mr. Harper,

The great thing about reading books is that it makes us better than cats. Cats are said to have nine lives. What is that compared to the girl, boy, man, woman who reads books? A book read is a life added to one's own. So it takes only nine books to make cats look at you with envy.

And I'm not talking here only of "good" books. Any book—trash to classic—makes us live the life of another person, injects us with the wisdom and folly of their years. When we've read the last page of a book, we know more, either in the form of raw knowledge—the name of a gun, perhaps—or in the form of greater understanding. The worth of these vicarious lives is not to be underestimated. There's nothing sadder—or sometimes more dangerous—than the person who has lived only his or her single, narrow life, unenlightened by the experience, real or invented, of others.

The book I am sending you today is a perfect instance of a story that offers you another life. It is a Bildungsroman (from the German, literally a "novel of education"), a novel that follows the moral development of its main character. Because it's told in the first person, the reader can easily slip into the skin, see through the eyes, of the person speaking. Jeanette Winterson's *Oranges Are Not the Only Fruit* is a brief 170 pages, but during those pages you become "Jeanette," the main character. Jeanette is a young woman who lives in small-town England a few decades ago. Her mother loves the Lord in a big way, and so does Jeanette. But the problem is, the problem becomes, that Jeanette also loves women in a big way. And those two—loving the Lord and loving women when you are yourself a woman—are not compatible, at least according to some who love the Lord and take it upon themselves to judge in His name.

Written in sparkling prose, *Oranges* is the sad, funny, tender tale of a young woman who must break into two pieces and then choose which of the two she wants to become. And that, having to make hard choices, having to choose between competing loves and lives, having to lose oneself so that one might find oneself, is instructive—besides highly entertaining—not only to adolescent Lancashire lesbians, but to me, to you, to everyone who is interested in making the most of life.

So enclosed, a fifteenth book, a fifteenth life.

Yours truly,
Yann Martel

P.S. Note the dedication. A book signed by the author herself. I had the good luck of meeting Jeanette Winterson in England recently and she kindly inscribed a copy of her book to you.

JEANETTE WINTERSON (b. 1959) is a British author and journalist. She shot to fame with the publication of her first novel, *Oranges Are Not the Only Fruit*, which won the 1985 Whitbread Prize for a First Novel. Since then, her novels have continued to push the boundaries of gender roles, sexual identity and imagination. Her continued contribution to British literature has earned her an Order of the British Empire. In addition to writing, Winterson owns a fine-food emporium, Verdes, in London.

BOOK 16

LETTERS TO A YOUNG POET
BY RAINER MARIA RILKE

November 12, 2007

To Stephen Harper,

Prime Minister of Canada,

These lessons from a wise and generous writer,

From a Canadian writer,

With best wishes,

Yann Martel

Dear Mr. Harper,

Rainer Maria Rilke's *Letters to a Young Poet*, the sixteenth book I am sending you, is a rich lode. These ten letters, written between 1903 and 1908 by the great German poet to a young man by the name of Franz Xaver Kappus, might be considered a precursor of creative writing instruction. They are useful to all of us who aspire to write. They have helped me, and I have no doubt that they will help you in the writing of your book on hockey.

For example, in the very first letter, Rilke asks the young poet to ask himself the vital question "Must I write?" If there is not that unstoppable inner necessity, then one should not even attempt to write, suggests Rilke. He also makes much of the need for solitude, for that quiet sifting of impressions from which comes good, true writing and which can occur only when one is on one's own.

However, if Rilke's letters were no more than technical advice on artful writing, I don't think I would have sent them to you. Of what interest is a trade manual to someone who prac-tices another trade? But these letters are much more than that, because what holds for art also holds for life. What illuminates the first illuminates the second. So, self-knowledge—must I write?—is useful not only in writing but in living. And solitude bears fruit not only for the one who aspires to write poetry but for anyone who aspires to anything. Whereas, to take a counter-example, I think it's rare that advice to do with commerce has much use beyond commerce. Our deepest way of examining life, of getting to our existential core, is through the artistic. At its best, such an examination has nearly a religious feel.

Take this passage towards the end of Letter Four, in which Rilke advises the Young Poet to wrap himself in solitude:

> Therefore, dear sir, love your solitude and bear with sweet-sounding lamentation the suffering it causes you. For those who are near you are far, you say, and that shows it is beginning to grow wide about you. And when what is near you is far, then your distance is already among the stars and very large; rejoice in your growth, in which you naturally can take no one with you, and be kind to those who remain behind, and be sure and calm before them and do not torment them with your doubts and do not frighten them with your confidence or joy, which they could not understand. Seek yourself some sort of simple and loyal community with them, which need not necessarily change as you yourself become different and again different; love in them life in an unfamiliar form and be considerate of aging people, who fear that being-alone in which you trust. Avoid con-tributing material to the drama that is always stretched taut between parents and children; it uses up much of the children's energy and consumes the love of their elders, which is effective and warming even if it does not comprehend. Ask no advice

from them and count upon no understanding; but believe in a love that is being stored up for you like an inheritance and trust that in this love there is a strength and a blessing. . . .

Doesn't this sound like a passage that Paul the Apostle might have written in one of his letters to the Corinthians?

Rilke's letters overflow with understanding, generosity and wise advice. They shine with loving kindness. Not surprising then that Franz Xaver Kappus wished so ardently to pass them on to posterity.

Yours truly,
Yann Martel

RAINER MARIA RILKE (1875–1926) was a poet and writer of lyrical prose. He was born in Prague, and studied in Germany. His works were heavily influenced by his studies in philosophy and his knowledge of Classic literature, and focus primarily on the themes of solitude and anxiety. Some of his most famous works include the *Sonnets to Orpheus*, the *Duino Elegies*, *Letters to a Young Poet* and *The Notebooks of Malte Laurids Brigge*. He was an avid traveller, and his journeys to France, Sweden and Russia, and the relationships he formed in those countries, marked his work. He died of leukemia.

BOOK 17

THE ISLAND MEANS MINAGO
BY MILTON ACORN
November 26, 2007

To Stephen Harper,
Prime Minister of Canada,
A book from an Island revolutionary,
From a Canadian writer,
With best wishes,
Yann Martel

Dear Mr. Harper,

Growing up, I was aware of the title that was popularly given to Milton Acorn: the People's Poet. I assumed that this was because his poetry was down-to-earth, the language plain, the meaning reaching into the accessible depths of common experience. What I hadn't realized until much later was that the People's Poet also had a political edge. That edge is made abundantly clear in the book that accompanies this letter, Acorn's *The Island Means Minago,* a varied collection of poems, personal essays and short plays. If you turn to the last pages of the book, you will find information on the publisher:

NC Press is the Canadian Liberation publisher. It is truly a people's publishing house, distributing books on the struggle for national independence and socialism in Canada and throughout the world.

On the next page, towards the bottom, there's also the following information:

NC Press is the largest Canadian distributor of books, periodicals, and records from the People's Republic of China.

An address is given for the organization behind both NC Press and its companion newspaper, New Canada:

Canadian Liberation Movement
Box 41, Station E, Toronto 4, Ontario

Was a revolutionary Canada ever a real possibility? Well, some people, way back in 1975, thought it was. Since then, I imagine the Canadian Liberation Movement has vanished, at least formally under that name, or if it still exists, that Box 41 is a peephole onto a lonely place.

But any revolution that uses poetry as one of its weapons has at least one correct thing going for it: the knowledge that artistic expression is central to who and how a people are. I wonder if the Fraser Institute has ever thought of publishing poetry to make its point, and if it hasn't, why not?

The portrait that Milton Acorn draws of Prince Edward Island, his native province, will likely be unfamiliar to you, as will be his reading of Canadian history. Let that be a reminder to you that the past is one thing, but what we make of it, the conclusions we draw, is another. History can be many things, depending on how we read it, just as the future can be many things, depending on how we live it. There is no inevitability to any historical occurrence, only what people will allow to take place. And it is by dreaming first that we get to new realities. Hence the need for poets.

So Milton Acorn was, of necessity as a poet, a dreamer (a tough one, mind you). He dreamt of a Canada that would be better, fairer, freer. He could not abide what he felt were the American shackles of capitalism and economic colonialism that held us down. He was an Island revolutionary. One might be inclined to smile at the extent to which some people's dreams are delusions. But better to dream than just to endure. Better to be bold than just to be told. Better to imagine many realities and fight for the one that seems best than just to shrug and retreat further into oneself.

The Island Means Minago represents yet another thing a book can be: a time capsule, a snapshot, a museum shelf of old dreams—that is, a reminder of a past future that never became (but is perhaps still worth dreaming about).

I'm making it sound as if *Minago* (Minago is the name the Mi'kmaq gave to P.E.I.) were nothing more than a political tract, which it is not. It is a book of poetry, a cry far richer than a tract. So I'll finish this letter the proper way, with one of Acorn's poems:

Bump, Bump, Bump Little Heart

Bump, bump, bump, little heart
along this journey
we've gone together,
you piping all the fuel.
You're fistsize, and fistlike
you clench and unclench,
clench and unclench
keeping this head upright
to batter its way
through the walls of the day.

Yours truly,
Yann Martel

MILTON ACORN (1923–1986), known as the People's Poet, had a seminal influence on Canadian literature. He was born in Charlottetown, and spent most of his life travelling between the growing literary scenes of Montreal, Toronto and Vancouver. He worked with many famous Canadian writers including Irving Layton, bill bissett, Al Purdy, Dorothy Livesay and Margaret Atwood. Acorn was a poetry-workshop instructor and founder of the *Georgia Straight*. He won the Canadian Poet's Award and the Governor General's Literary Award for *The Island Means Minago*. Other famous works include *Dig Up My Heart* and *Jawbreakers*.

BOOK 18

METAMORPHOSIS
BY FRANZ KAFKA

December 10, 2007

To Stephen Harper,
Prime Minister of Canada,
A cautionary tale of sorts,
From a Canadian writer,
With best wishes,
Yann Martel

Dear Mr. Harper,

The book that accompanies this letter is one of the great literary icons of the twentieth century. If you haven't already read
it, you've surely heard of it. The story it tells—of an anxious,
dutiful travelling salesman who wakes up one morning trans-
formed into a large insect—is highly intriguing, and therefore
entertaining. The practical considerations of such a change—
the new diet, the new family dynamic, the poor job prospects,
and so on—are all worked out to their logical conclusion. But that
Gregor Samsa, the salesman in question, nonetheless remains at
heart the same person, the same soul, still moved by music, for
example, is also plainly laid out. And what it all might mean,
this waking up as a bug, is left to the reader to determine.

Franz Kafka published *Metamorphosis* in 1915. It was one of his
few works published while he was alive, as he was racked by
doubts about his writing. Upon his death in 1924 of tuberculosis, he asked his friend and literary executor, Max Brod, to destroy

all his unpublished works. Brod ignored this wish and did the exact opposite: he published them all. Three unfinished novels were published, *The Trial*, *The Castle* and *Amerika*, but in my opinion his many short stories are better, and not only because they're finished.

Kafka's life, and subsequently his work, was dominated by one figure, his domineering father. A coarse man who valued only material success, he found his son's literary inclinations incomprehensible. Kafka obediently tried to fit into the mold into which his father squeezed him. He worked most of his life, and with a fair degree of professional success, for the Workers' Accident Insurance Institute of the Kingdom of Bohemia (doesn't that sound like it's right out of, well, Kafka?). But to work during the day to live, and then to work at night on his writings so that he might feel alive, exhausted him and ultimately cost him his life. He was only forty years old when he died.

Kafka introduced to our age a feeling that hasn't left us yet: angst. Misery before then was material, felt in the body. Think of Dickens and the misery of poverty he portrayed; material success was the road out of that misery. But with Kafka, we have the misery of the mind, a dread that comes from within and will not go away, no matter if we have jobs. The dysfunctional side of the twentieth century, the dread that comes from mindless work, from constant, grinding, petty regulation, the dread that comes from the greyness of urban, capitalist existence, where each one of us is no more than a lonely cog in a machine, this was what Kafka revealed. Are we done with these concerns? Have we worked our way out of anxiety, isolation and alienation? Alas, I think not. Kafka still speaks to us.

Kafka died seven months into the public life of Adolf Hitler—the failed Munich Beer Hall Putsch, in which the ugly Austrian corporal had prematurely tried to seize power, took place in

November of 1923—and there is something annunciatory about the overlap, as if what Kafka felt, Hitler delivered. The overlap is sadder still: Kafka's three sisters died in Nazi concentration camps.

Metamorphosis makes for a fascinating yet grim read. The premise may bring a black-humoured smile to one's face, but the full story wipes that smile away. One possible way of reading *Metamorphosis* is as a cautionary tale. So much alienation in its pages makes one thirst for authenticity in one's life.

Christmas is fast approaching. I'll see with the next book I send you if I can't come up with something cheerier to match the festive season.

Yours truly,
Yann Martel

FRANZ KAFKA (1883–1924) was born in Prague, Bohemia (now the Czech Republic), and is considered one of the most influential authors of the twentieth century. Much of Kafka's work is disturbing, dealing with nightmarish situations and dark themes including alienation, dehumanization and totalitarianism, a literary style now known as "Kafkaesque." He is best known for his novella *Metamorphosis* as well as for two of his novels, *The Trial* and *The Castle*, which were published posthumously. He earned a doctorate in law and wrote in his spare time, spending most of his working life at an insurance company.

THE BROTHERS LIONHEART
BY ASTRID LINDGREN

IMAGINE A DAY
BY SARAH L. THOMSON AND ROB GONSALVES

THE MYSTERIES OF HARRIS BURDICK
BY CHRIS VAN ALLSBURG

December 24, 2007

To Stephen Harper,
Prime Minister of Canada,
Three books to make you and your family dream,
From a Canadian writer,
With best wishes,
Yann Martel
P.S. Merry Christmas

Dear Mr. Harper,

It is Christmas tomorrow, and we live in a country where the first-mentioned fundamental freedom in the Charter of Rights is the freedom of conscience and religion. It is a time to celebrate. But curious how, despite the vast, lawful liberty that is ours to enjoy, we Canadians are so constricted in our religious expression. So "Merry Christmas!" is fast disappearing from public greetings, replaced by formulations such as "Happy Holidays" or "Holiday Greetings," which are held to be safely generic, the original meaning of holiday—holy day—being conveniently forgotten.

Yet "Merry Christmas" is just a blessing being offered. Does it offend? Would you or I be offended, actually offended, if someone shouted to us, "Happy Diwali!" or "Happy Hanukkah!" or "Happy Eid!" with a smile and a wave of the hand? Wouldn't we rather be gratified by the well-wisher's kind intentions, even if we are not Hindu, Jewish or Muslim? Similarly, when we gift a "Merry Christmas" to a stranger—and how good it is to reach out to strangers—is our intention not kind? Our spiritual stomach is full, so to speak, and we are offering blessed food to another. If that person should reply, "Thank you! Blessed be your Baby, my Prophet thought most highly of him," we don't take offence that their stomach is already full. In fact, we are happy for them. Better an abundance of food than a lack, no?

I love it that one religious group stops working, halts the making of money, to celebrate the birth of a baby. We tend to forget babies too much, I think. We tend to neglect magical thinking.

Most of our compatriots take their religious freedom as meaning they are free not to practice any religion, and they address life with big questions and big myths they get elsewhere. That's fine. To each his or her own path.

But it's Christmas tomorrow, I repeat, and by all accounts you are a Christian, and rightly entitled to say "Merry Christmas," though you are far more discreet about your Christianity than your predecessor as party leader, the Honourable Stockwell Day. It made people uncomfortable, his liberal use of his constitutionally given religious freedom. You are more savvy and cautious. You seem to be somewhat of a closet Christian, not speaking much or sharing much of Jesus of Nazareth.

Still, it's Christmas tomorrow and there's a Baby to be celebrated.

So, in the spirit of the occasion, I offer you this time not one book, but three, and books not to be read alone, like an adult, but to be shared with children. *The Mysteries of Harris Burdick*, by Chris Van Allsburg, and *Imagine a Day*, written by Sarah L. Thomson and illustrated by Rob Gonsalves, are picture books of contagious magic. You will look at them, at each page, and marvel. *The Brothers Lionheart* (pardon the terrible cover—it's the only edition I could find), by Astrid Lindgren, of the famous Pippi Longstocking series, is a novel for children with fewer illustrations, and black and white, but it is just as magical. I hope you and your family enjoy all three books.

Merry Christmas, Mr. Harper. May your heart be the manger in which the newborn Baby lies.

Yours truly,
Yann Martel

ASTRID LINDGREN (1907–2002) was a Swedish author best remembered for her contributions to children's literature, particularly the beloved Pippi Longstocking and Karlsson-on-the-Roof series. Her stories have been translated into dozens of languages and are read around the world. During her career, she received the Hans Christian Andersen Award and the Right Livelihood Award. After her death, the government of Sweden created an award in her name to honour outstanding achievement in children's and youth literature.

SARAH L. THOMSON was formerly a senior editor at HarperCollins Children's Books. After publishing her first book, *The Dragon's Son*, she resigned from her editorial position in order to pursue writing full-time. To date she has written twenty children's titles and won several awards, including the 2005 Oppenheim Toy Portfolio Gold Seal Award for *Amazing Tigers!* and a Bank Street College of Education Best Book of the Year award for *Amazing Gorillas!*

ROB GONSALVES (b. 1959) is a Canadian painter whose style is described as both surrealist and magical realist. His art is characterized by fantastical and detailed optical illusions, transforming the ordinary into the extraordinary. He has worked as an architect, muralist and theatre painter, experiences that are reflected in his paintings of buildings and landscapes. Though he is not primarily a children's illustrator, he has worked on the children's books *Imagine a Day*, *Imagine a Night* and *Imagine a Place*.

CHRIS VAN ALLSBURG (b. 1949) is an American author and illustrator of children's books, most notably *Jumanji* and *The Polar Express*. His fantastical stories are set in incredible places and feature magical, dangerous or mysterious objects. Van Allsburg is known for exploring themes in his stories that are darker than those usually associated with children's literature. He has also collaborated as an illustrator with other authors, including illustrated editions of C. S. Lewis's *Chronicles of Narnia*. He has won the Caldecott Honor Medal several times.

BOOK 20

THE EDUCATED IMAGINATION
BY NORTHROP FRYE

January 7, 2008

To Stephen Harper,
Prime Minister of Canada,
A book that defends the essential,
From a Canadian writer,
With best wishes,
Yann Martel

Dear Mr. Harper,

I hope you and your family had a good Christmas and that you are returning to work with your mind and heart refreshed. I suspect 2008 will be a busy year for us. I have a book to finish and you have a government to run. We both hope to get good reviews for our respective labours.

I was in Moncton in late November last year, doing a series of special events organized by the Northrop Frye Literary Festival, which runs every year in April. Someone asked me, in a lovely Acadian accent, "As-tu lu *The Educated Imagination* de Northrop Frye?" ("Have you read . . .")

I hadn't read Frye's *The Educated Imagination*. Or anything else by him. Northrop Frye—and I'm educating myself as I tell you what follows, catching up—lived between 1912 and 1991, spending his early formative years in Moncton (hence the name of the festival) and most of his adult years at the University of Toronto, where he was a great light. Frye was a world-class literary critic who wrote such books as *Fearful Symmetry: A Study of William Blake*, *Anatomy of Criticism* and *The Great Code: The Bible and Literature*. He led a thrilling life of the mind, most of it fed by literature, and he gave much to his students and readers. He was a great thinker, teacher, Canadian.

I should explain why I have never until now read Frye. It wasn't intellectual sloth. It was rather a conscious decision. Frye, as I've just said, was a literary critic. He looked at literature, he looked *through* literature, seeing in it recurring symbols, underlying structures, overarching metaphors. All of which is no doubt fascinating—but not to the young man I was when I started writing. Self-knowledge is often a good thing—it teaches you your limits—but too much of it too soon can ruin the incipient artist in you if it gives you the sense that you have no original core, that you are just dough in a pre-established mould. Then, as now, I just wanted to write, to create, to invent. I wasn't interested in being told what I was doing, whom I was repeating, what convention I was adhering to. Why become self-conscious if it meant I wouldn't dare to write? So I avoided literary criticism, those words and books that might snuff out my wavering creative flame. Trope was tripe to me.

However, right after being asked the question by the person with the lovely Acadian accent, I was presented by her with the book in question, Northrop Frye's *The Educated Imagination*. She thought of it because of the small book club you and I have going. She wondered if you might not enjoy it (you may be interested to know that I get suggestions of books to send you all the time). I felt it would be rude not to read so considerate a gift. And surely, with three books completed and a fourth one nearly done, I could withstand a literary critic suddenly turning a mirror on me.

Well, I'm happy to report that I read the book and I'm still standing. *The Educated Imagination* was interesting to me, and I think it might be even more interesting to you. Frye, in this short, oral book—he delivered it in six parts as the 1962 Massey Lectures—speaks about the role of literature in education and society, about whether the first is needed by the other two.

It certainly is needed, Frye argues persuasively. It all comes down to language and the imagination. Frye explains that no matter what use we are making of language, whether it's for practical self-expression, to convey information or self-consciously to be creative, we must use our imagination. As he puts it: "Literature speaks the language of the imagination, and the study of literature is supposed to train and improve the imagination. But we use our imagination all the time: it comes into all our conversation and practical life: it even produces dreams when we're asleep. Consequently we have only the choice between a badly trained imagination and a well trained one, whether we ever read a poem or not." Imagination is not just for writers. It's for everyone. At another point, Frye says, "The fundamental job of the imagination in ordinary life . . . is to produce, out of the society we have to live in, a vision of the society we want to live in." This statement has obvious political implications. You see why I said this book might be of interest to you.

One of the classic dualities of existence is that of the head and the heart, of thinking and feeling, of reason and emotion. It's not untrue, but I do wonder how useful this division is. One might suppose that a mathematician hard at work is being entirely reasonable while someone crying at the scene of a terrible accident is being entirely emotional, but otherwise can we so clearly delineate between the two? Frye believed that these are rather different ways of using one's imagination, that the imagination underpins them both. And the better, the more fertile our imagination, the better we can be at being both reasonable and emotional. As broad and deep as our dreams are, so can our realities become. And there's no better way to train that vital part of us than through literature.

The imagination, then, is where is all starts, both for you and for me.

Happy New Year.

Yours truly,
Yann Martel

NORTHROP FRYE (1912–1991) was one of Canada's most respected literary critics and theorists. He gained international notoriety for his first book, *Fearful Symmetry,* and continued to establish his reputation with *Anatomy of Criticism* and *The Stubborn Structure.* Frye was a member of the Royal Society of Canada and a Companion of the Order of Canada. During his lifetime, he won several awards including the Lorne Pierce Medal, the Pierre Chauveau Medal and the Governor General's Literary Award. Apart from his significant contributions to Canadian literature, his name is also a frequent crossword puzzle clue and he is honoured each year at a literary festival in Moncton.

BOOK 21

THE CELLIST OF SARAJEVO
BY STEVEN GALLOWAY

January 21, 2008

To Stephen Harper,
Prime Minister of Canada,
A whole-person work,
From a Canadian writer,
With best wishes,
Yann Martel

Dear Mr. Harper,

You may have asked yourself on occasion what process I go through to select the books I have been sending you. Why don't I answer that question in this letter.

Any book adheres to one convention or another—be it that of the Novel or the Biography—and all sentences are either conventionally grammatical or conventionally ungrammatical. It's the rare, very rare writer who is genuinely unconventional, and usually their revolution is at one level only, affecting, say, point-of-view, while following the herd when it comes to punctuation. A writer who is unconventional on too many levels runs the risk of losing the reader, who can't manage to get a solid footing on so much new territory and gives up the effort. *Finnegans Wake,* by the Irish writer James Joyce, is an example of such arduous total newness.

A book is a convention, then, as are the categories of thinking that produce books: Art, History, Geography, Science, and so on. That's how we like it, we humans. We like orderly sentences and orderly books in much the same way we like orderly streets and orderly governments. Which is not to say that we are not bold creatures. We are; in fact, there is no bolder creature on Earth. To give you a non-literary example: in the late 1960s, the Americans marshalled together the conventions of science, engineering, management and financing, and as a result achieved the highly unconventional goal of popping two of their citizens onto the Moon.

Back to books. They are products of convention, but there are many conventions. I mentioned two already, the Novel and the Biography, which flow from two other conventions, Fiction and Non-fiction. Within each, there are sub-conventions, categories, genres. I have tended to send you books of fiction rather than non-fiction because fiction is a more worked-through interpretation of life. What do I mean by that? I mean that fiction is both more personal and more synthesized than non-fiction. Fiction is more whole-person. A novel is about Life itself, whereas a history remains about a specific instance of Life. A great Russian novel—remember the Tolstoy I sent you—will always have a more universal resonance than a great history of Russia; you will think of the first as being about you on some level, whereas the second is about someone else.

So that's the first rule: a work of fiction. Now, there are many *kinds* of fictions. There is the literary novel, the thriller, the murder mystery, the satire, and so on. As you haven't yet communicated to me your literary interests, and since it's not for me to judge what you should read, I have not excluded any genre. Whatever book I send you must only be good; that is, once you've read it, you must feel wiser, or at least more knowledgeable. Or to put it another way, as I did many months ago, it must increase your sense of *stillness*.

The other considerations are simple:

1) I send you short books, generally under two hundred pages. You are probably busier than most people, and you probably feel that you are more importantly busy. I believe that's an illusion. As a friend once told me, the only thing that will really go down in history is how we raise our children. The life of the Canadian people is determined and built by each and every Canadian, one small act at a time. There are twenty-four hours in a day and each one of us chooses how to fill those hours. No one's hour is more important than anyone else's. Nonetheless, it's harder to follow an eight-hundred-page tome in fifteen-minutes snatches than it is a slim novel.

2) For the same reason that you likely don't give yourself stretches of hours in which to wrap your mind around a convoluted story, I send you books that speak plainly.

3) I send you books that are varied, that will show you all that the word can do. At the rate of one book every two weeks, this is a harder requirement to satisfy. There are *so* many good books out there, Mr. Harper. But I must pace myself. I am starting with older books, aiming to be foundational, and from there I will build up to books from our comparatively young nations of Canada and Quebec.

Within those broad criteria, I choose the books I send you in a spontaneous, nearly random way, just whatever strikes me as possibly of interest to you. I also listen to the suggestions of others, as I did two weeks ago with Frye's *The Educated Imagination*. (Did you enjoy it, by the way?)

But some rules are meant to be broken, and this week's book is an example of that. Steven Galloway's novel *The Cellist of Sarajevo* speaks plainly, but it's a little too long by our criteria (fifty-eight pages over the limit), it's Canadian and it's so recent that it qualifies as prenatal: it hasn't even been published yet. It's supposed to come out in April of this year. The unadorned paperback you have in your hands is what publishers call an advance reading copy. It's sent out to booksellers, journalists and book clubs to drum up interest and excitement in a book prior to its publication—sort of like politicians doing the summer barbecue circuit before an election. The general reading public does not normally see an advance reading copy. What you are holding in your hands is a rare item.

And it's also a grand and powerful novel about how people retain or reclaim their humanity when they are under extreme duress. I'm sure you will hear about *The Cellist of Sarajevo* from other people than just me. It's set during the brutal siege of the Bosnian city of Sarajevo in the early 1990s. That story was in the news for years, yet I think most of us just took it in dumbly, wondering how people could do that to each other. Well, Galloway's novel explains how. It does the work of a good fiction: it transports you to a situation that might be alien to you, makes it familiar, and so brings understanding. That's what I meant when I said fiction is "whole-person." While reading *The Cellist of Sarajevo* you are imaginatively there, in Sarajevo, as the mortar shells are falling and snipers are seeking to kill you as you cross a street. Your mind's eye sees, your moral sense is outraged: your full humanity is being exercised.

Yet *The Cellist* is a directed and digested take on reality, it's not journalism. There is subtle intent woven into the realistic narrative of its three main characters. You will see that when you read the last line of the novel, which is magnificent.

Yours truly,
Yann Martel

Steven Galloway (b. 1975) is a Canadian novelist whose work has been translated into more than twenty languages. Besides *The Cellist of Sarajevo*, he has written the novels *Finnie Walsh* and *Ascension*. Galloway teaches creative writing at Simon Fraser University and the University of British Columbia.

BOOK 22

MEDITATIONS
BY MARCUS AURELIUS
February 4, 2008

To Stephen Harper,
Prime Minister of Canada,
A book from a fellow head of government,
From a Canadian writer,
With best wishes,
Yann Martel

Dear Mr. Harper,

Like you, Marcus Aurelius was a head of government. In AD 161, he became Emperor of Rome, the last of the "five good emperors"—Nerva, Trajan, Hadrian, Antoninus Pius, Marcus Aurelius—who ruled over an eighty-four-year period of peace and prosperity that lasted from AD 96 to 180, the Roman Empire's golden apogee.

The case of Rome is worth studying. How a small town on a river became the centre of one of the mightiest empires the world has known, eventually dominating thousands of other small towns on rivers, is a source of many lessons. That Rome was mighty is not to be doubted. The sheer size the empire achieved is breathtaking: from the Firth of Forth to the Euphrates, from the Tagus to the Rhine, spilling over into Northern Africa, for a time the Romans ruled over most of the world known to them. What they didn't rule over wasn't worth having, they felt: they left what was beyond their frontiers to "barbarians."

Another measure of their greatness can be found in the Roman influences that continue to be felt to this day. Rome's local lingo, Latin, became the mother language of most of Europe, and Italian, French, Spanish and Portuguese are still spoken all over the world. (The Germanic hordes beyond the Rhine, meanwhile, have managed to sponsor only one international language, albeit a successful one, English.) We also owe the Romans our calendar, with its twelve months and 365-and-a-quarter-day years; three days in our week hark back to three Roman days—Moonday, Saturnday and Sunday; and though we now use the Roman number system (i, ii, iii, iv, v, vi . . .) only occasionally, we use their 26-letter alphabet constantly.

Despite their power and might, another lesson about the Roman Empire forces itself upon us: how it's all gone. The Romans reigned far and wide for centuries but now their empire has vanished entirely. A Roman today is simply someone who lives in Rome, a city that is beautiful because of its clutter of ruins. Such has been the fate of all empires: the Roman, the Ottoman, the British, the Soviet, to name only a few European empires. Which will be the next empire to fall, the next to rise?

The interest in reading Marcus Aurelius's *Meditations*, the book I am sending you this time, lies as much in their content as in the knowledge of who wrote them. European history has got us used to seeing one monarch after another reach the throne for no reason other than direct filial relation, with talent and ability playing no role. Thus the unending line of mediocre personalities—to put it charitably—who came to rule and mismanage so many European nations. This was not Marcus Aurelius's route to power. Although he inherited the throne from Emperor Antoninus Pius, he was not Pius's biological son.

Nor was he elected. He was rather selected. Roman emperors did pass on their emperorship to their sons, but this linkage was rarely directly biological. They instead designated their successors by a system that was authoritarian yet flexible: adoption. Marcus Aurelius became emperor as a result of being adopted by the reigning emperor. Each emperor chose whom he wanted as his successor from among the many capable and competing members of Rome's diverse elite class. Members of that class were often related, but they still had to prove themselves if they wanted to move up in the world.

In that, Roman society was much like the modern democracies of today, with an educated, principled elite that sought to perpetuate the system and, with it, itself. The Rome of then, in some ways, doesn't seem so different from the Ottawa, Washington or London of today. After the alien abyss, frankly, that is much European history, with the Europeans thinking and behaving in ways that are close to unfathomable by contemporary standards, it is a surprise to see, nearly two thousand years ago, a people who thought and fought and squabbled and had principles which they squandered, and so on—why, a people seemingly just like us. Hence the endless interest of Roman history.

So Marcus Aurelius was a man of great ability selected to be Roman emperor. In other words, he was a politician, and, like you, a busy one; he spent much of his time battling barbarian hordes on the frontiers of the empire. But at the same time, he was a thinking man—with a penchant for philosophy—who put his thoughts down on the page. He was a writer.

Emperor Marcus Aurelius was a Stoic and some of his pronouncements are on the gloomy side: "Soon you will have forgotten the world, and soon the world will have forgotten you," is a fairly typical pronouncement of his. There is much made in these meditations on the ephemerality of the body, of fame, of empires, of pretty well everything. Over and over, Marcus

Aurelius exhorts himself to higher standards of thinking and behaving. It's bracing, salutary stuff. In many ways, it's the perfect book for you, Mr. Harper. A practical book on thinking, being and acting by a philosopher-king.

It's also not the sort of book one reads right through from page 1 to page 163. It has no continuous narrative or developing argument. The *Meditations* are rather self-contained musings divided into twelve books, each book divided into numbered points that range in length from a single sentence to a few paragraphs. The book lends itself to being dipped into at random. My suggestion is that each time you open and read it, you put a dot next to the meditations you read. That way, over time, you will read all of them.

Yours truly,
Yann Martel

MARCUS AURELIUS (121–180 CE) wrote his *Meditations* in Greek while on military campaigns during 170–180 CE. In them, he stresses the importance of government service, duty, endurance, abstinence, surrendering to Providence and achieving detachment from things beyond one's control.

BOOK 23

ARTISTS AND MODELS
BY ANAÏS NIN
February 18, 2008

To Stephen Harper,
Prime Minister of Canada,
Hot stuff,
From a Canadian writer,
With best wishes,
Yann Martel

Dear Mr. Harper,

Valentine's Day was just a few days ago and we've had a long cold snap here in Saskatchewan—two good reasons to send you something warming.

Anaïs Nin—such a lovely name—lived between 1903 and 1977 and she was the author of a number of novels that remain unknown to me: *Ladders to Fire*, *Children of the Albatross*, *The Four-Chambered Heart*, *A Spy in the House of Love* and *Solar Barque* form a five-volume *roman-fleuve* entitled *Cities of the Interior* (1959). She also published the novels *House of Incest* (1936), *The Seduction of the Minotaur* (1961) and *Collages* (1964), and a collection of short stories, *Under a Glass Bell*. The only pleasure these have given me has been to wonder what they are about. What story would a novel called *Solar Barque* tell? What was the *Albatross* and who were her *Children?*

Nin is better known for her published diaries, which covered every decade of her life except the first (and she missed that one only by a year, since she started her diary when she was eleven years old). She was born in France, lived in the United States for many years, she was beautiful and cosmopolitan, and she came to know many interesting and famous people, the writer Henry Miller among them, all of whom she discussed and dissected in her diary. Her diary's importance lies in the fact that female voices have often been silenced or ignored—still are—and an extended female monologue covering the first half of the twentieth century is rare.

And Anaïs Nin also wrote erotica. Hot stuff. Kinky stuff. Pages full of women who are wet not because it's raining and men who are hard not because they're cruel. *Artists and Models*, which contains two stories from her collections of erotic writings *Delta of Venus* and *Little Birds*, is the latest book I'm sending you. It may leave you cold, Mr. Harper, reading about Mafouka the hermaphrodite painter from Montparnasse and her lesbian roommates or about the sexual awakening of a painter's model in New York, but it bears noting that while covering our loins and our hearts with clothes is often useful—it's minus 23 degrees Celsius outside as I write these words—there is the risk that they are also hiding, perhaps burying, an essential part of us, one that does not think but rather feels. Clothes are the commonest trappings of vanity. When we are naked, we are honest. That is the essential quality of these lustful stories of Nin, embellished or wholly invented though they may be: their honesty. They say: this is part of who we are—deny it, and you are denying yourself.

Yours truly,
Yann Martel

ANAÏS NIN (1903–1977) was born in Paris, raised in the United States and identified herself as a Catalan-Cuban-French author. Nin was a prolific novelist, short story writer and diarist, best known for her multi-volume *Diary*. She was also one of the greatest writers of female erotica, and is famous for her affairs with notable individuals including Henry Miller and Gore Vidal.

BOOK 24

WAITING FOR GODOT
BY SAMUEL BECKETT
March 3, 2008

To Stephen Harper,
Prime Minister of Canada,
A modernist masterpiece,
From a Canadian writer,
With best wishes,
Yann Martel

Dear Mr. Harper,

Curiously, the book that I am sending you this early March, a play, only the second dramatic work I've sent you, is one that I don't actually like. It has always irked me. Which is not to say that it is not a good play, indeed, a great play. In fact, that it continues to irk me confirms its greatness in a way, because if I said to you confidently, "This is a masterpiece," that would imply I had a settled view of it, a fixed understanding, and that the play stood for me like a statue on a pedestal: lofty, staid and undisturbing. Samuel Beckett's *Waiting for Godot* is none of these.

To further confirm that I'm wrong in my view of *Godot*, I'll say that despite being written in the late 1940s, the play will not feel dated when you read it. This is a significant achievement. Plays, to state the obvious, are made up of dialogue. There is no surrounding prose to supply context. You might think the setting of a play would be the equivalent of the description in a novel that sets up the story, but that is not the case. Many historical plays and operas are restaged in settings that their playwrights and composers would never have imagined, and no meaning is lost. Shakespeare's *Macbeth* does not need a castle in the background to make sense to theatregoers. The meaning and development of a play is entirely carried on the shoulders of its dialogue. But the way we speak changes over time, and quickly words and expressions that were current to the playwright sound old-fashioned to us today.

Moreover, plays are exclusively concerned with relationships, with the feelings between characters, revealed in what they say to each other and how they behave, and some relationships have also changed over the course of history. Lastly, plays are precisely, literally situated, the actors wearing costumes and moving about settings that we actually see, as opposed to imagining them in prose. How these last two points make most plays a more perishable product than most prose will be made clear if you think back to old television shows. Do you remember the 1970s American television series *Bewitched*, Mr. Harper, about a witch named Samantha who lives in suburbia with her husband, Darrin, and their daughter, Tabitha? I lapped it up when I was a kid. A few years ago I happened to see an episode again—and I was appalled. The sexism struck me as egregious, what with Darrin always trying to prevent Samantha from using her magic and Samantha, being the good, docile housewife, always trying to comply. And the way they dressed and their hairdos—that at least was innocently laughable. You get my point. What was fresh and funny then is now old and embarrassing. Women are now more free to use their magic, and we dress differently. By capturing so exactly a time, a place and a lingo, many plays are as fleeting as newspapers.

It is a mighty playwright who manages to speak to his or her time and also to ours. Shakespeare does it, toweringly. That a student doesn't know what a "thane" is, that kings don't rule in 2008 the way they ruled in 1608 in no way affects the power and meaning of the Scottish play today. *Waiting for Godot* has also managed to speak to all times, so far. Despite premiering in 1953, the antics, musings and worries of Vladimir and Estragon will likely strike you as funny, puzzling, insightful, maddening and still current.

The play is about the human condition, which in Beckett's pared-down vision of it means that the play is mostly about nothing. Two men, the ones just mentioned, Didi and Gogo familiarly, wait around because they believe they have an appointment with a certain Godot. They wait around and talk and despair, are twice interrupted by two crazies by the names of Pozzo and Lucky, and then they go back to waiting around, talking and despairing. That's pretty well it. No plot, no real development, no final point. The setting is also mostly nothing: just a single, solitary tree along an empty country road. The only props of note are boots, bowler hats and a rope.

Essentially, two hours of nothing that's good and deep, pessimistic and funny. Beckett meant to strip away at the vanities of our existence and look at the elemental. Therein lies what makes *Waiting for Godot* both great and eye-rolling as far as I'm concerned. There is this line, for example, said by I can't remember which character: "We give birth astride a grave." I suppose that's true. Death interrupting life, what value can life have? If we must eventually let go of everything, why take hold of anything to start with? This sort of pessimism is the burden of those who have witnessed terrible times (Beckett lived in France during the German occupation) and the delight of undergraduates in the throes of youthful angst. I realize that my life is no more durable than a leaf's, but between when I'm fresh and gloriously atop a tree and when I'll be yellow and raked away by Time, there are some good moments to be had.

Samuel Beckett was with the same woman, Suzanne Beckett, *née* Deschevaux-Dumesnil, for over fifty years. And he was apparently an avid fan and player of tennis. In these two attachments, I see a contradiction between what the man wrote and how he lived. If he had the joy and energy to whack a bouncy yellow ball over a net, if he had the joy and comfort of knowing that someone was there for him at the end of each day, what was he so desperate about? A wife and tennis—how much more did he expect from life? And this is aside from exploring the ideas of those who dismiss death as a mere threshold, just a gap you have to mind between the train of life and the platform of the eternal.

Still, I know *Waiting for Godot* is a great play. You'll see that when you read it. It's a masterpiece. It does what no play did before it.

Yours truly,
Yann Martel

SAMUEL BECKETT (1906–1989) was an Irish author, playwright and poet, and is considered one of the last modernists or possibly one of the first post-modernists. Beckett's writing was characterized by minimalism and black humour. He lived in France, and worked as a courier in the French Resistance during World War II. He was awarded the Nobel Prize in Literature in 1969. His best known novels are *Molloy, Malone Dies* and *The Unnamable*.

BOOK 25

THE DRAGONFLY OF CHICOUTIMI
BY LARRY TREMBLAY
March 17, 2008

To Stephen Harper,
Prime Minister of Canada,
This play to defeat silence,
From a Canadian writer,
With best wishes,
Yann Martel

Dear Mr. Harper,

It's about time I sent you the work of a writer from English
Canada's twin solitude. It's a play again, the second in a row,
the third in all. And for the second time—*Le Petit Prince* was
the first—I am sending you a book in French. Mind you, the
French of Larry Tremblay's *The Dragonfly of Chicoutimi* is a
bit peculiar. Not that it's *joual*, or any other variation of Quebec
French; that wouldn't be peculiar, it would be expected from a
Québécois play. Rather, if you glance at the text, you will think
it's just English, plain and simple. Well, it's not. Tremblay's
play is a play written in French—that is, thought, felt, ordered,
and expressed by a French mind—only using English words.

What's the point of that? Is this a bit of stand-up comedy,
some party trick drawn out into a play? It's not. The cover of
the book will tell you as much. Do you recognize the man on
it? It's Jean-Louis Millette, the great actor who died just a few
years ago, far too soon. His arms are raised, his face expresses

anguish, the background is black: this play is no joke, says the cover. *The Dragonfly of Chicoutimi* is indeed a serious work of art, premiered and reprised by a master.

Is the point of writing a play that is French in its nature but English in its appearance political? The answer to that question might be yes, but a tenuous yes, in that any work of art can be taken to have political implications. In this case, to read the play politically I think diminishes its scope. Larry Tremblay's play is both far too personal—it's the monologue of a man opening up his heart about a private matter—and far too universal to be reduced to a political tract about the survival of the French language in Quebec.

I think Tremblay means to signal the political neutrality of his play when Gaston Talbot, the man who is opening up his heart, says of himself:

> once upon a time a boy named Gaston Talbot
> born in Chicoutimi
> in the beautiful province of Quebec
> in the great country of Canada
> had a dream . . .

In describing both entities, and with adjectives of equal banality—if not cliché in the case of Quebec, officially "La Belle Province"—my guess is that Tremblay sought to place his play's linguistic dualism beyond a merely political interpretation. The dream mentioned, by the way, is not a political dream, but a dream about Gaston Talbot's mother, whose love he seeks.

So what has Gaston Talbot from Chicoutimi got to say, and why is he saying it in French rendered in English?

I would suggest that *The Dragonfly of Chicoutimi* is a play about suffering and redemption, about what we have to do to get back to ourselves. Gaston Talbot is an adult French-speaking man struck with aphasia who, when we meet him, suddenly begins to speak again, only in English rather than in his native tongue. And what he recounts is how, long ago, he was a sixteen-year-old boy in love with a twelve-year-old boy by the name of Pierre Gagnon-Connally and how the two went by the river bank to play and Pierre asked Gaston to be his horse and Pierre

> . . . catches me
> with an invisible lasso
> inserts in my mouth an invisible bit
> and jumps on my back
> he rides me guiding me with his hands on my hair
> after a while he gets down from my back
> looks at me as he never did before
> then he starts to give me orders in English
> I don't know English
> but on that hot sunny day of July
> every word which comes
> from the mouth of Pierre Gagnon-Connally
> is clearly understandable
> Get rid of your clothes
> Yes sir
> Faster faster

And then something happened, it's not clear what, an accident, an inexplicable burst of violence, and Pierre Gagnon-Connally dies and Gaston Talbot falls into silence.

The play is a web of self-confessed lies and inventions. The first thing Gaston Talbot says is "I travel a lot." Later, he admits that he hasn't travelled anywhere. In recounting a dream, he first says that he had one face, a "Picasso face," then admits that it was another face. Gaston Talbot holds these lies up like a shield, and with them he edges forward towards the truth. English words are thus just one more of these truth-revealing lies that allow him to address what pushed him into the worst abyss of all: silence.

As I did for the fourth book I sent you, *By Grand Central Station I Sat Down and Wept*, by Elizabeth Smart, I would suggest that you read *The Dragonfly of Chicoutimi* aloud. Even better: that you read it silently a first time, as if you were Gaston Talbot before the start of the play, and then read it a second time aloud, as if you were Gaston Talbot gasping for expression.

The play of course raises the question of language and identity, of what it means to speak in one language rather than another. Languages obviously have cultural reference points, but these can change. Witness English, spoken, taken on fully, by so many people around the world who are not of English culture. But the play puts the question on a more personal level. Gaston Talbot manages to reach back into his painful past and say what he has to say thanks to a bilingual subterfuge. That is the startling and moving conclusion of the play: the sight of truth found through a mask.

Yours truly,
Yann Martel

LARRY TREMBLAY (b. 1954), born in Chicoutimi, is a Québécois poet, novelist, non-fiction writer, playwright, stage director, actor and teacher. His plays often explore psychic and social violence, and showcase his use of vivid imagery and his signature crisp, rhythmic style.

BOOK 26:

BIRTHDAY LETTERS
BY TED HUGHES
March 31, 2008

To Stephen Harper,
Prime Minister of Canada,
This collection of great poems to celebrate
the one-year anniversary of our book club,
From a Canadian writer,
With best wishes,
Yann Martel

Dear Mr. Harper,

We are celebrating a birthday, you and I. The book that accompanies this letter is the twenty-sixth that you have received from me. Since I have been sending you these literary gifts every two weeks, that means that our cozy book group is celebrating its first anniversary. How have we done? It's been a most interesting odyssey, taking more of my time than I expected, but the pleasure has kept me keen and motivated. The result, so far, is a folder with copies of twenty-six letters for me and a shelf with twenty-eight slim books for you (a discrepancy owing to the fact that I sent you three books for Christmas). If we look over your new, growing library, we see:

13 novels
3   collections of poetry

3 plays
4 books of non-fiction
4 children's books, and
1 graphic novel

written (or, in one case, edited) by:

1 Russian
5 Britons
7 Canadians (including 1 Québécois)
1 Indian
4 French
1 Colombian
2 Swedes
3 Americans
1 German
1 Czech
1 Italian, and
1 Irish

of whom:

16 were men
9 were women, with
2 books authored by both sexes, and
1 book authored by writers of unknown sex (though my
guess is that the *Bhagavad Gita* was written by men)

Too many novels, too many men, not enough poetry, why
haven't I sent you a Margaret Atwood or an Alice Munro yet—
at the rate of a book every two weeks, it's hard to be representative and impossible to please everyone. But we're getting
there. Glenn Gould once said, "The purpose of art is the lifelong construction of a state of wonder." There is time yet.

It seemed appropriate on this anniversary occasion to offer you a book entitled *Birthday Letters*. It has the celebratory word in the title, even if the tone of the book does not exactly evoke a cake with a small lit candle on it.

The facts are as follows. In 1956, a twenty-six-year-old Englishman named X married a twenty-three-year-old American woman named Y. They had two children. Their relationship proved fraught with tensions, made worse by X's affair with a woman named Z, and in 1962 X and Y separated. In 1963, Y, mentally unstable since her teenage years, committed suicide by gassing herself. Six years later, in 1969, Z, who by then had a child with X, a little girl nicknamed Shura, also killed herself, unpardonably taking Shura with her. Two last facts: first, by virtue of being still married to Y when she died, X became her testamentary executor, and, second, X was constant throughout his life in his infidelities.

The amount of pain contained within these anonymous facts—the torment, the heartache, the sorrow, the shame, the regret—is barely conceivable. What life would not be overwhelmed, utterly destroyed, by such pain? And would that pain not be made worse if it were displayed for the whole world to see and comment upon?

X was Ted Hughes, Y was Sylvia Plath and Z was Assia Wevill, and their collective pain, the terrible mess that was their lives, would have been lost and forgotten had not the first two been superb and well-known poets who gave expression to that pain. Further notoriety was added by the fact that sides could easily be taken with this tragedy. Why does tragedy so often make us take sides? I guess because strong emotions move us, and we move to one side or another, so to speak, as if fleeing a car that is out of control, and it takes the passage of time, the examination of memory, for us to look back with calm sorrow, standing steadily, no longer so inclined to move and take sides. At any rate, it doesn't take a lawyer to detect conflict of interest in Hughes being the literary executor of Plath, her pained posthumous collections of poetry and her pained journals being edited by the very man who caused a good deal of her pain, some say editing her works with an eye to improving his reputation. That he furthermore destroyed the last volume of her journal, the one chronicling the last months of their relationship, only makes the charge against him more credible. And what to think of his incessant promiscuity? Who could imagine that shame and regret would so little curb libido?

Sides were taken, vociferously. Hughes was scorned and hated until his death by feminists and Plath-lovers, and I doubt the controversy of their relationship will ever slip from public interest. What stands in Hughes's defence? That question has an easy answer. His poetry.

That the author of *Birthday Letters* might be portrayed as a callous philanderer, arrogant and remorseless, is irrelevant in the face of the magnificence of his poetry. It reminds one of the fact that great art is, in its essence, not moral but testimonial, bearing witness to life as it is honestly lived, in its glorious heights as well as in its turpitudinous depths.

Great poetry tends to shut up the novelist in me. It takes so many words to make a novel, reams and reams of sentences and paragraphs, and then I read a single great poem, not even two pages long, and all my prose feels like verbiage. You will see what I mean when you read these poems. They are narrative poems, the tone intimate, usually an "I" speaking to a "you," the language quicksilver, extraordinarily concise, simple words arranged in an original and forceful way, and the result, poem after poem, is not only a clear image but an unforgettable impression. Take "Sam," or "Your Paris," or "You Hated Spain," or

"Chaucer," or "Flounders," or "The Literary Life," or "The Badlands," or "Epiphany," or "The Table."

Ted Hughes was perhaps, if one is in the sanctimonious mood to judge, a bastard, but the bastard was also an amazing bard, his poetry dazzling. And the evidence from *Birthday Letters* is clear: X really did love Y, so if art can redeem, here is redemption.

Yours truly,
Yann Martel

TED HUGHES (1930–1998) was a children's writer, dramatist, short story writer, critic and acclaimed poet, holding the position of British Poet Laureate from 1984 until his death. Hughes's earlier poetry, including his first collection, *Hawk Roosting,* focused on beauty and violence in nature, while his later collections, like *Crow,* were existential, satirical and cynical. He wrote more than ninety books, and received a Guggenheim fellowship, the Whitbread Prize for Poetry and the Order of Merit.

BOOK 27

TO THE LIGHTHOUSE
BY VIRGINIA WOOLF

April 14, 2008

To Stephen Harper,
Prime Minister of Canada,
From a Canadian writer,
With best wishes,
Yann Martel

Dear Mr. Harper,

Your classic this week is a somewhat harder read than most of the other books I have sent you. Many books are direct and frontal in their approach; immediately upon starting them, a reader senses what the author wants to talk about. To take an example from the books on your shelf, we are immediately familiar with the setting of George Orwell's *Animal Farm,* even if we've never lived on a farm, and we see right away his allegorical intent. We appreciate that a real event, the tragedy of Soviet Russia under Stalin, is going to be examined by means of a fable set on an imaginary farm. Armed with that understanding, animated by certain expectations, we read on.

Books such as these, the majority of books I'd say, create a subtle interplay of familiarity and strangeness. The familiar brings the reader onboard, and then the strange takes that reader somewhere new. The two elements are necessary. A book that proves to be entirely familiar is boring. Even the most formulaic of genre fiction attempts to convey some feeling of uncertainty and then, only at the very end, reassures the reader that every-thing is as he or she would wish it to be, the boy getting the girl or the detective catching the murderer. Conversely, a book can't be entirely strange, otherwise the reader would have no entry point, would flounder and give up.

Virginia Woolf's *To the Lighthouse,* published in 1927, will have you floundering a bit. Please don't give up. For me, it starts working, it takes you in, on about the twentieth page (that is, on page 29 of the edition I'm sending you). Before that, you'll be puzzled, perhaps even vaguely annoyed. So many characters coming and going, no clear plot in sight, tangents and digres-sions aplenty—where is the clarity and pace of good old Victorian literature? What is Woolf up to?

Well, it's anyone's guess—good literature is forever open to interpretation—but by my reckoning Woolf is exploring at least two things here:

1) She is exploring the mind, how consciousness interacts with reality. Woolf's experience of it, one that I'm sure will be familiar to you, is of intent buffeted by intrusion, like a salmon swimming upstream. Her characters think, but their thinking is constantly interrupted by events that are either external in their origin—other characters coming up—or internal, the mind distracting itself from its own thinking. I'm sure you've heard of the term "stream of conscious-ness," Woolf's narrative technique is like that. What she is exploring in *To the Lighthouse* isn't so much an ordered series of events—although those are present in the novel—as the mind filtering those events.

2) She is exploring time, the effect and experience of it, which explains why the novel is given its cadence not by

the regular, objective tick-tock of a clock, but instead by the subjective reactions of the characters to time, which goes by slowly when the characters are engrossed, and then seems to leap forward years in a blink. Isn't that how time is for all of us, both crawling and leaping, like a frog's progress. Those two animal images might help you as you read the book. Try to recognize the salmon and the frog in *To the Lighthouse*.

Woolf's prose is dense, detailed and repetitive, but in a mesmerizing way. Not surprisingly, another of Woolf's novels is called *The Waves*. Her novel is like that, lulling and mysterious.

It's always nice to know a little about the author of a book. Virginia Woolf was English. She was born in 1882 and she died in 1941 by suicide. She was mad at times and mad most of the time; that is, she was periodically plagued by mental illness and she was always angry at the limitations placed upon women. Virginia Woolf was a bold, experimental writer and a feminist figurehead of great importance.

One indication both of Woolf's literary approach and of her character is her fondness for the semi-colon. The period is final and unsubtle, might be termed masculine. The comma, on the other hand, is feminine as some men might want women to be, indefinite and subservient. Woolf instead favours the punctuation mark that most resembles where she wanted to be as a writer and as a woman, a mark like a sluice gate, one that is more open than the period but more in control than the comma, a feminist punctuation mark. Woolf famously wrote an essay called *A Room of One's Own,* in which she describes the difficulties of being a female writer in a field dominated by men. Well, her prose is like that, full of thoughts that are related but wouldn't fit in the oppressive big room of a single sentence;

they rather inhabit the many smaller rooms of a sentence punc-
tuated by semi-colons.

I invite you to enter slowly, mindfully, taking your time, the
many rooms of Virginia Woolf's prose.

Yours truly,
Yann Martel

VIRGINIA WOOLF (1882–1941) was a prolific British writer, publishing over five hundred essays and dozens of novels, short stories and
non-fiction books. *A Room of One's Own*, her most famous non-fiction
composition, discusses the issue of women writing in a male-dominated
society and why few women in her time were successful novelists. Other
celebrated works include *To the Lighthouse*, *The Waves* and *Orlando*. She
was married to the writer Leonard Woolf, and together they founded
and operated the Hogarth Press, which published works by T.S. Eliot,
Katherine Mansfield and John Maynard Keynes, and introduced British
readers to Sigmund Freud's work on psychoanalysis. Woolf committed suicide when she was fifty-nine, most likely because of undiag-
nosed bipolar disorder.

BOOK 28

READ ALL ABOUT IT!
BY LAURA BUSH AND JENNA BUSH

April 28, 2008

To Stephen Harper,
Prime Minister of Canada,
A book from two pillars of society,
From a Canadian writer,
With best wishes,
Yann Martel

Dear Mr. Harper,

This is an unusual book I am sending you, for a number of reasons. For starters, it's fresh off the press. I bought it the day it was published. None of that pleasing, comforting wornness to it, like an old friend coming for a visit. Instead, a shiny, spine-cracking, new-smelling newness. And it's a children's book, not something I'd normally send to an adult.

What won me over to this book was its theme and the profession of its authors. *Read All About It!* is about the appeal and the importance of reading. Tyrone Brown, the protagonist, a student at Good Day Elementary School, is good at math, good at science, good at sports, but he doesn't like reading. When Miss Libro brings the kids to the school library to read to them, Tyrone is soooooo bored. He'd rather daydream. But one day, when Miss Libro is reading from a book about an astronaut, he pays attention—and he's taken in. Suddenly his world changes. It becomes populated by ghosts and dragons and historical figures like Benjamin Franklin (this is an American book) and, most endearingly, by a pig. Tyrone comes to realize that books are a fantastic way to dream. I won't tell you the rest of the story. You'll have to read all about it yourself.

The authors, Laura Bush and Jenna Bush, a mother-daughter team, are teachers and, according to their bios on the backflap, "passionate about reading."

A word about teachers. I love teachers. I always have. If I were not a writer, I'd be a teacher. I cannot think of a more important profession. It has always struck me as odd that lawyers and doctors should have such high standing—reflected not only in their salaries but in their social prominence—when, in the course of a normal, happy, healthy life, one should only exceptionally have to consult either. But teachers—we've all met and needed teachers. Teachers shaped us. They came into our dark minds and lit a light. They taught us both explicitly and by example. To teach is a magnificent verb, a social verb, imply-ing someone else, whereas the verbs to earn, to buy, to want are lonely and hollow.

I could name so many of the teachers who marked my life. In fact, I will. Miss Preston and Mrs. Robinson were two of my early homeroom teachers. Mr. Grant taught me biology. Mr. Harvey taught me Latin. Mr. McNamara and Sister Reid taught me mathematics. Mr. Lawson and Mr. Davidson taught me English. Mr. Van Husen and Mr. Archer taught me history. The amazing Mr. Saunders taught me geography. And so on. Three decades have gone by, and still I remember these people. Where would I be without them, what frustrated, angry soul would I be? There is only so much parents can do to form us. After that, our fate lies with teachers.

And when we are no longer full-time students, there are all the informal teachers we meet as adults, the men, women and children who know better and who show us how to do better, how to be better.

Pity, then, that we live in a society that so little values teachers and schools. We have, alas, Mr. Harper, fallen upon times in which the common thinking seems to be that societies should be run as if they were corporations, with profitability as the guiding imperative. In this corporatist view of society, those who do not generate dollars are deemed undesirable. So it is that rich societies become unkind to the poor. I see this mean attitude in my own beloved province of Saskatchewan, where the new government is waging, as I've heard it put, a "war on the poor," and this, at a time of unprecedented prosperity [which is ongoing in Saskatchewan, despite the global economic crisis; we are a "have" province]. As if the poor will just disappear if ignored enough. As if there will be no broader consequence to the poor becoming poorer. As if the poor aren't citizens too. As if some of the poor aren't helpless children.

Well, in this race in which they are left behind, the poor are joined by students. Because investing in the education of a six-year-old, with a return that will be seen only in fifteen years or so, once that student has got a job and has started paying taxes, is not an investment worth making if one is looking to make quick money. And so we fund our schools minimally, burdening university students with levels of debt that neutralize their ability to be wealth-generating citizens. How can you buy a car, a house, appliances, how can you contribute to the economy, if you're crushed by a massive debt? The corporatist agenda is thus defeated by its own ideology.

Teachers are at the forefront of resisting this negative trend. With whatever means they are given, until they burn out, as they too commonly do, they continue their effort to produce intelligent, knowledgeable, caring citizens. Teachers are pillars of society.

Most teachers are women, certainly at the elementary school level, just as most readers are women. Laura Bush and Jenna Bush, teachers and readers both, are in that way typical. One is left wondering: while wives and daughters are teaching and reading, what are husbands and fathers doing? In our society, does the left hand know what the right hand is doing?

Yours truly,
Yann Martel

LAURA BUSH (b. 1946), wife of former president George W. Bush, taught elementary school and worked as a school librarian. She is a founder of the National Book Festival, and honorary chair of the Laura Bush Foundation for America's Libraries. During her husband's presidential terms, she was honoured by the Elie Wiesel Foundation for Humanity and the American Library Association. Her daughter JENNA HAGER (née Bush) (b. 1981) is also an elementary school teacher. In 2007, Jenna wrote *Ana's Story: A Journey of Hope*, chronicling her experiences with UNICEF in South America.

BOOK 29

DROWN
BY JUNOT DÍAZ
May 12, 2008

To Stephen Harper,
Prime Minister of Canada,
A bottle with ten genies in it,
From a Canadian writer,
With best wishes,
Yann Martel

Dear Mr. Harper,

The book that accompanies this letter was heartily recommended to me by a bookseller. I'd never heard of it or of its author. I thought to myself, Well, why not? An obscure book that moved at least one reader. That makes it as valid as a book that moved a million. A little later, I mentioned my choice to a friend and she said, "Oh, he just won the Pulitzer Prize two days ago."

So much for the obscurity of Junot Díaz. I'm sending you *Drown*, his first book, a collection of short stories. It came out in 1996. It took Díaz eleven years to write his second book, the novel *The Brief Wondrous Life of Oscar Wao*, for which he won, just a month ago, the Pulitzer.

That's one of the good things about literary prizes. They bring attention to books or authors that might otherwise be missed by readers. The life of the literary writer is mostly invisible, like the movement of lava under the surface of the earth. Poems, short stories and novels are published, they are reviewed here and there, sales are modest, the world forgets, the writer writes on. It sounds dull, it's generally financially impoverishing, but hidden from view is the intoxication of being creative, the wrestling with words, the heaven of good writing days, the hell of bad ones, with at the end of it the sense that one has proven King Lear wrong, that something *can* come of nothing. A book is a bottle with a genie inside it. Rub it, open it, and the genie will come out to enchant you. Imagine being the one who put the genie in the bottle. Yes, it's terribly exciting work.

However, the world is strewn with such bottles, and many don't get much rubbing. Sometimes that's right, sometimes it's unfair. Only time will tell. Meanwhile, the writer continues to labour.

Then, one day, you are told that five readers liked your book. And they're the right readers, because they're on the jury of a prize. In fact, they've decided to give you the prize. Suddenly the clouds of the book world part and you hear a booming voice say, "This is my son, whom I love; with him I am well pleased." You're ceremoniously hauled out of obscurity. It's not an unpleasant experience, far from it. I'm grateful for every nod I've ever received.

But if I won, doesn't it mean that someone lost? That's the less appealing part of it, the feeling that you've become a racehorse, that you are competing, that there are winners and losers. History may decree that it is so, but it's not how it feels on the inside. On the inside, you're alone in your shop with your bottle and your genie.

Back to Junot Díaz. *Drown* is a collection of ten short stories, ranging in length from six to thirty-nine pages. These are the first short stories I've sent you. You'll find the experience quite different from reading novels. You'll be changing gears more often, so to speak. Díaz is a Dominican-American and his stories cover what it means to have a hyphen in one's identity, the potential for it to be a gulf, a dream, a strain, a loss. The English is peppered with Spanish, the tone is oral and informal, the characters profane and touching. It's a world of kids left to themselves, where there's no money and no father, no jobs and no prospects, only streets and harried mothers, drugs and fickle relations.

Now how will these stories expand your stillness, you might ask, the stillness with which life is properly examined? The answer might be found in the following quote from the story "Boyfriend," about a couple breaking up. The man comes by a few times to pick his stuff up:

> She let him fuck her every time, maybe hoping that it would make him stay but you know, once someone gets a little escape velocity going, ain't no play in the world that will keep them from leaving. I would listen to them going at it and I would be like, Damn, ain't nothing more shabby than those farewell fucks.

The toughness is surface. Beneath it is hurt and questioning. People are people, just trying to get by and make sense of things. No matter the language or the posing, the yearning for stillness is the same.

Yours truly,
Yann Martel

JUNOT DÍAZ (b. 1968) is a Dominican-American novelist and short story writer. He and his family moved to New Jersey when he was six years old. His first novel, *The Brief Wondrous Life of Oscar Wao,* is his best-known work; it has earned him several awards including the National Book Critics Circle Award and the 2008 Pulitzer Prize, and has been optioned for film. Díaz currently teaches creative writing at MIT and is the fiction editor at the *Boston Review.*

BOOK 30

THE KREUTZER SONATA
BY LEO TOLSTOY
May 26, 2008

To Stephen Harper,
Prime Minister of Canada,
Music, both beautiful and discordant,
From a Canadian writer,
With best wishes,
Yann Martel

Dear Mr. Harper,

Tolstoy again. Sixty weeks back I sent you *The Death of Ivan Ilych,* if you remember. This week it's *The Kreutzer Sonata,* published three years later, in 1889. A very different book. As much as *Ilych* is an artistic gem, the realism seemingly effortless, the characters fully incarnate yet universal, the emotions finely expressed, the lyricism simple and profound, the portrayal of life and its fleetingness dead on, so to speak—in sum, as much as *Ilych* is perfect, *The Kreutzer Sonata* is imperfect. For example, the setting—a long train ride in which two passengers converse—comes off poorly because nearly the entire novella is taken up by the endless discourse of the main character, Pozdnyshev. Our nameless narrator just sits there, stunned into listening and memorizing the 75-page tirade directed at him. It's as clunky a device as one of Plato's dialogues—without the wisdom, for the most part. *The Kreutzer Sonata* is a long rant about love, sex and marriage, with sideswipes at doctors and children, leading up to a vivid portrayal of insane jealousy, all of it told by an unconvicted murderer. Imagine that, a man telling you on a train, "I killed my wife. Let me tell you about it, since we've got all night." I guess I wouldn't interrupt him, either.

Imperfect art, then. So why the interest? Because it's still Tolstoy. Simple people lead simple lives. Complex people lead complex lives. The difference between the two has to do with one's openness to life. Whether determined by misfortune—a congenital deficiency, a stunting upbringing, a lack of opportunity, a timid disposition—or determined by will—by the use and abuse of religion or ideology, for example—there are many ways in which life, one's portion of it, can be regulated and made acceptably simple. Tolstoy was unregulated. He lived in a manner unbridled and unblinkered. He took it all in. He was supremely complex. And so there was much of life in his long life, life good and bad, wise and unwise, happy and unhappy. Thus the interest of his writings, because of their extraordinary existential breadth. If the earth could gather itself up, could bring together everything upon it, all men, women and children, every plant and animal, every mountain and valley, every plain and ocean, and twist itself into a fine point, and at that fine point grasp a pen, and with that pen begin to write, it would write like Tolstoy. Tolstoy, like Shakespeare, like Dante, like all great artists, is life itself speaking.

But whereas *Ilych* elicits consonance in the reader, *The Kreutzer Sonata* elicits dissonance. In it, love between men and women does not really exist but is merely a euphemism for lust. Marriage is covenanted prostitution, a cage in which lust unhappily fulfills itself. Men are depraved, women hate sex, children are a burden, doctors are a fraud. The only solution is complete sexual abstinence, and if that means the end of the human species, all the better. Because otherwise men and women will always be unhappy with each other, and some men may be driven to killing their wives. It's a bleak, excessively scouring view of the relations between the sexes, a reflection of Tolstoy's frustration at the social constrictions of his times, no doubt, but nonetheless going too far, wrong-headed, objectionable. And so its effect, the scandal upon its publication, and the reaction it has to this day. Tolstoy does indeed go too far in *The Kreutzer Sonata*, but in it are nonetheless expressed all the elements—the hypocrisy and the outrage, the guilt and the anger—that were at the core of that greatest revolution of the twentieth century: feminism.

As an aside, this second book by Tolstoy was a last-minute choice. There's such a world of books out there to share with you that I thought one book per author as introduction was enough. After that, if you were interested, you could look up for yourself any given author's other books.

Only I wanted a book this week that touched on music. (I've forgotten to explain the title of Tolstoy's novella. Pozdnyshev's wife is an amateur pianist. The couple meets an accomplished amateur violinist by the name of Trukhashevsky, a man. The wife and he become, in all innocence, friends because of their mutual fondness for music. They decide to play Beethoven's Kreutzer Sonata, for piano and violin, together. In the wings, her husband grows angrier.) Why a book on music? Because serious music, at least as represented by new and classical music, is fast disappearing from our Canadian lives. I have belatedly learned of the latest proof of this: the CBC Radio Orchestra is to be disbanded. Already our public radio's fare of music has been paltrified. There was once, Mr. Harper, a show called *Two New Hours* on CBC, hosted by Larry Lake. It played Canadian new music. Its last slot, surely the least desirable for any show, was on Sundays between 10 p.m. and midnight, too late for the early birds, too early for the night owls. Airing at that time, no surprise that few people managed to listen to it. When I did, though, I was grateful. New music is a strange offering. It is, as far as I can tell, music that has broken free. Free of rules, forms, traditions, expectations. Frontier music. New world music. Anarchy as music. Which might explain the screechy violins, the pianos gone crazy, the weird electronic stuff.

I have intense memories of listening to *Two New Hours* and doing nothing but that. Because really, it's impossible to read while your radio is sounding like two tractors mating. I suppose I'm more jaded when it comes to writing—jaded, jealous, bored, whatever. But I listened to *Two New Hours* out of pure curiosity. And I was surprised, moved and proud that there were creators out there responding to our world in such fresh and serious ways. Because it was clear to me: this was serious stuff, strange as it sounded. This was music that, under whatever guise, was the voice of a single person trying to communicate with me. And I listened, thrilled at the newness of it. That is, I listened until the show was cancelled.

And now the CBC Radio Orchestra, the last radio orchestra in North America, is to be similarly cancelled. No more, "That was _____, played by the CBC Radio Orchestra, conducted by Mario Bernardi," as I heard for years. Who will play us our Bach and Mozart now, our R. Murray Schafer and Christos Hatzis?

It amazes me that at a time when Canada is riding the commodities wave to unprecedented wealth, with most levels of government experiencing budgetary surpluses, that we are ridding ourselves of a piddly little orchestra. If this is how we are when in fortune, how will we be when in misfortune?* How

---

* The CBC Radio Orchestra was indeed disbanded at the end of November 2008. It is now trying to survive as the National Broadcast Orchestra, on a budget of one million dollars a year, peanuts compared to the money Western

much culture can we do *without* before we become lifeless, corporate drones?

I believe that both in good and bad times we need beautiful music.

Yours truly,
Yann Martel

economies have lost thanks to incompetent bankers and politicians. We are now poorer in every way, with less classical music coming to us from the radio and less money in our pockets.

BOOK 31

THEIR EYES WERE WATCHING GOD
BY ZORA NEALE HURSTON

June 9, 2008

To Stephen Harper,
Prime Minister of Canada,
An incandescent novel,
From a Canadian writer,
With best wishes,
Yann Martel

Dear Mr. Harper,

Some voices are barely heard. They are left to speak among themselves, worlds within worlds. Then someone listens, gives them artistic expression, and now the loss is lesser, because those voices have become eternal. Such is the achievement of the American writer Zora Neale Hurston (1891–1960) with her masterpiece *Their Eyes Were Watching God*. You will notice the language right away. There are two voices in the novel. One is the narrative voice that frames the story. It is lyrical, metaphor laden and formal. Take the first two paragraphs of the novel:

Ships at a distance have every man's wish on board. For some they come in with the tide. For others they sail forever on the horizon, never out of sight, never landing until the Watcher turns his eyes away in resignation, his dreams mocked to death by Time. That is the life of men.

Now, women forget all those things they don't want to remember, and remember everything they don't want to forget. The dream is the truth. Then they act and do things accordingly.

The other voice is that of the characters, and it's something else. They speak in the African-American vernacular, and you'll hardly believe that English can do such things. A random example:

> "Well, all right, Tea Cake, Ah wants tuh go wid you real bad, but,—oh, Tea Cake, don't make no false pretense wid me!"
> "Janie, Ah hope God may kill me, if Ah'm lyin.' Nobody else on earth kin hold uh candle tuh you, baby. You got de keys to de kingdom."

It's not cute, it's not folkloric, it's not patronizing. The effect is rather of a renewal of language. You read—you hear—as if you were hearing for the first time. And what you will hear is the story of Janie Crawford, a black woman whose voyage of self-discovery, with its hard-earned lessons, is told through her three marriages.

The most significant element in the life of Zora Neale Hurston—even greater than that she was a woman—was that she was black. It is inconveivable that her writing—consisting of four novels, two books of folklore, an autobiography and more than fifty shorter pieces—would have been the same had she been white. She was black in a white society that for two hundred years had held blacks in slavery. She was black in a society that was, at best, racial in its thinking, and, at worst, racist. I imagine that every day of her life there was some glance, some exchange, some limitation that reminded Hurston of the colour of her skin and what that was held to mean.

Now, it's hard, when you are perpetually made aware of one single element of your identity, be it the colour of your skin, the shape of your body, your sexual orientation, your ethnic heritage, whatever, not to linger and dwell on that element, not to become twisted and bitter as a result. Yet the miracle of Hurston's art is that it manages not to linger and dwell, not to be twisted and bitter. *Their Eyes Were Watching God* is not a diatribe about racist America, though examples of racism are easily found in it. It is instead an incandescent novel about a character whose full humanity and destiny is explored—and she happens to be black.

I suspect that if you read the first chapter of *Their Eyes Were Watching God*, you'll read the other nineteen. You will read about Janie and Tea Cake, about love and muck, about happiness and disaster. And the worth of that—other than that you will have been entertained—is that for the duration of a story you will have entered the being of an African-American woman. You will have heard voices that you might otherwise never have heard.

Yours truly,
Yann Martel

P.S. One of the joys of buying secondhand books is the unexpected treasures they sometimes contain. Case in point: a colour photo slipped out of your copy of Their Eyes *when I opened it. A group shot. Nothing written on the back. Nine people camping: five women, three men, and one girl in a lifejacket. Though no doubt casually taken, note what an excellent photo it happens to be, how the way the people are arranged is aesthetically pleasing, the eye moving in an easy circle from the seated woman on the left to the girl on the right, how the group is slightly off-centre so that the feel of the shot is unstudied, how the peripheral elements are unobtrusive yet revealing. It struck me that the group is shaped in the form of an eye. We think we're looking at them, but, in fact, they are an eye looking out at us, winking. Perhaps that's why they're smiling, amused at the trick they're playing on us, the viewer being viewed. I wonder what the story of these people is. Clearly they're a family. Was this their book? Who among them read it? What stories do they have, what voices?*

ZORA NEALE HURSTON (1891–1960) was part of the Harlem Renaissance of the 1920s. She published four novels, two books of folklore, an autobiography and more than fifty essays, articles, short stories and plays. Her most famous novel, *Their Eyes Were Watching God*, is written in a fluid and expressive vernacular, a bold stylistic choice that gave new literary voice to African-Americans. There was a revived interest in her work following a 1975 article published in *Ms. Magazine* by Alice Walker about Hurston's writings.

BOOK 32

THE REZ SISTERS
BY TOMSON HIGHWAY

June 23, 2008

To Stephen Harper,
Prime Minister of Canada,
From a Canadian writer,
With best wishes,
Yann Martel

Dear Mr. Harper,

So far, if there is one thing that your administration has done that will stand the test of time, it is the formal apology to the victims of the Canadian government's Native residential school system. Policies come and go, are changed and forgotten, but an apology stands. An apology changes the course of history. It is the first step in true healing and reconciliation. I congratulate you on this important symbolic gesture.

Since your mind was recently on Canada's original inhabitants—and since National Aboriginal Day was just two days ago—it's appropriate that I should send you Tomson Highway's play *The Rez Sisters*. It too is of historical importance. Of the author, there's an unusually long bio at the start of the book, a full four pages, so you can read there about the life of Tomson Highway, at least until 1988, when the play was published.

What is not mentioned in the bio is the synergy that developed in the Aboriginal cultural world in Toronto in the mid-1980s. Suddenly then—the time was right—some Natives came together and did what they had hardly done until then: they spoke. The production company Native Earth Performing Arts was founded in 1982 to give voice to Aboriginal theatre, dance and music. Before that, with the exception of Inuit prints and sculptures and Maria Campbell's memoir *Half-Breed*, the Canadian cultural scene was practically bare of Native expression. That would change with Native Earth. Along with Tomson Highway, the company fostered the careers of such writers as Daniel David Moses and Drew Hayden Taylor.

When *The Rez Sisters* opened in November 1986, the cast had to go out into the streets and beg passersby to come in and see the play. Well, those first people liked what they saw and word of mouth did the rest. *The Rez Sisters* became a hit. It drew large audiences, toured the country, was produced at the Edinburgh Theatre Festival.

Like your last book, Zora Neale Hurston's *Their Eyes Were Watching God*, the force of *The Rez Sisters* lies with its characters. Seven women—Pelajia Patchnose, Philomena Moosetail, Marie-Adele Starblanket, Annie Cook, Emily Dictionary, Veronique St. Pierre and Zhaboonigan Peterson—live on the Wasaychigan Hill Indian Reserve, on Manitoulin Island. Life there is as life is everywhere, with its ups and downs. But then comes momentous news: THE BIGGEST BINGO IN THE WORLD is being organized in Toronto. And do you know what kind of a jackpot THE BIGGEST BINGO IN THE WORLD would have? Something BIG. The dreams that winning that jackpot might fulfill is at the heart of the play. It's a comedy, the kind that makes you laugh while also delivering a fair load of sadness. Stereotypes are set up and then mocked, but it's not an overtly political play, hence its universal resonance. We may not be Native women on a reserve, we may not be bingo aficionados, but we all have dreams and worries.

There is a last character in the play who must be mentioned. Nanabush, in his various incarnations, is as important in Native mythology as Christ is in the Christian world. But there's a playful element to Nanabush that is absent in our portrayal of Christ. In *The Rez Sisters,* he appears in the guise of a seagull or a nighthawk. He dances and prances and pesters. Marie-Adele, who has cancer, and Zhaboonigan, who was brutally raped, are the only ones who explicitly interact with him. He is the angel of death, but also the spirit of life. He hovers over much of the play.

Yours truly,
Yann Martel

TOMSON HIGHWAY (b. 1951) is a Cree author and playwright who is best known for his plays *The Rez Sisters* and *Dry Lips Oughta Move to Kapuskasing,* both winners of the Dora Mavor Moore Award. He is also the author of the bestselling novel *Kiss of the Fur Queen.* Highway's writing features Native characters living on reserves and incorporates Native spirituality. He continues to advocate for Native issues and expose the injustices and challenges faced by the Native Canadian population. Highway is a talented concert pianist and an entertaining stage presence, and is currently producing his third play, *Rose.*

BOOK 33

PERSEPOLIS
BY MARJANE SATRAPI
July 7, 2008

To Stephen Harper,
Prime Minister of Canada,
This armchair trip to the Islamic Republic of Iran,
From a Canadian writer,
With best wishes,
Yann Martel

Dear Mr. Harper,

In the mid-1990s, I travelled to Iran with a young woman. In the two months we were there, we met maybe twenty Western travellers, all of them with transit visas and all speedily making their way along the central corridor that passes through Iran from the border of Turkey to the border of Pakistan. We were specifically interested in Iran, not in getting from Europe to Asia, so we had managed to get tourist visas. We wandered all over the country, visiting not only Teheran, Esfahan and Shiraz, cities you will have heard of, but others, too: Tabriz, Rasht, Mashhad, Gorgan, Yazd, Kerman, Bandar Abbas, Bam, Ahvaz, Khorramabad, Sanandaj. (Sorry for the long list of names; they may mean nothing to you, but each one opens up a volume of memories in me.) We also visited Zoroastrian fire temples in the desert. We climbed an ancient ziggurat. We took ferries to islands. We rested in oases.

I've often found that, excluding war zones, a foreign place is never so dangerous as when you are far away from it. The closer you get to it, the more the distortions caused by fear and misunderstanding dissipate, so that, to take the case at hand, the image we had of the Islamic Republic of Iran, that terrifying place that brought the world full-on religious fanaticism, with oppressed women going about dressed from head to toe in black and people flagellating themselves in public and fountains spewing blood-red water, disappeared once we entered the country and was replaced by this or that friendly individual standing in front of us, eyeing us with curiosity, wanting to be kind but uncertain of his or her English.

If Iran was challenging, it was in the way it challenged our expectations. For example, in all our time there, talking freely to men and women of all social classes, from the rural poor to the urban middle class, from the devout to the secular, we never met, not once, a person who complained about living in an Islamic republic. A government has to be a mirror into which its people can look and recognize themselves. Well, the Iranians we met recognized themselves in their Islamic democracy. The only complaint we heard, and often, was about the state of the economy. Iranians complained about lacking money, not lacking freedom.

There wasn't much to do in Iran in the way of leisure then. It was, by Western standards, and probably still is, an arid society, with little space or money given over to cinemas, concert halls, sports complexes and the like. And there were no bars or discos, of course. Iran was a sober place, both literally and metaphorically. So Iranians did the only thing they could easily: they socialized. As a result, they are a people with the most graceful and sophisticated social skills I've ever seen, a people who, when they meet you, really meet you, turning their full attention to you. The Iranians we met were open, curious, generous, extraordinarily hospitable and endlessly chatty.

And the horrors of fundamentalism? The people who brought us Salman Rushdie's fatwa? The oppression of women? That's all true, too. But what place is above censure? People in Iran are like people anywhere: they want to be happy and live in peace, with a modicum of material well-being. The rules of their society, their values—the means by which they hope to become happy—are different from Canada's, but what of that? They have their problems, we have ours. Let them muddle through theirs, as we hope to muddle through ours. Progress can't be jump-started; it must arise organically from within a society, it cannot be imposed from without.

Such eye-opening travel as I had the luck of doing isn't a possibility for everyone. Work, family and inclination may prevent one from ever visiting this or that foreign place. Which is where books come in. The armchair traveller can be as well informed as the backpacker roughing it, so long as he or she reads the right books. Travel, whether directly with one's feet or vicariously through a book, humanizes a place. A people emerge in their individual particularity, miles away from caricature or calumny.

And so *Persepolis,* by Marjane Satrapi. It's a graphic novel, the second I've sent you after *Maus,* by Art Spiegelman. It's charming, witty, sad and illuminating. The point of view is that of a ten-year-old girl named Marjane. She's like all ten-year-olds the world over, living in her own half-imaginary universe—only it's 1979 and she lives in Iran. A revolution is afoot, one that will be welcomed at first by her middle-class family because it will bring down the odiously corrupt and brutal regime of the Shah, but later will be hated because of the excesses that followed. It's a story that has the ring of truth to it because it's the story of an individual telling it as she saw it.

I invite you to read *Persepolis* and get a hint of the Iran I visited some years ago. If you enjoy it, you should know that there's a *Persepolis 2,* which continues Marjane's story, and there's also a movie.

Yours truly,
Yann Martel

MARJANE SATRAPI (b. 1969) is a multi-talented Iranian-French author. She is primarily a graphic novelist but also writes and illustrates children's books. She is best known for her popular autobiographical graphic novel *Persepolis,* and its sequel, *Persepolis 2.* In these books, she recalls her childhood growing up in Iran and her adolescence studying in Europe. *Persepolis* won the Angoulême Coup de Coeur Award and was later adapted into an animated film recognized at the Cannes Film Festival. Satrapi studied illustration in Strasbourg and lives in France.

BOOK 34

THE BLUEST EYE
BY TONI MORRISON

July 21, 2008

To Stephen Harper,
Prime Minister of Canada,
From a Canadian writer,
With best wishes,
Yann Martel

Dear Mr. Harper,

Oh, the mess that the heart wreaks. The pity of it all when so much was possible. Toni Morrison's novel *The Bluest Eye* is unbelievably short—a mere 160 pages—considering all that it carries of pain, sadness, anger, cruelty, dashed hopes, of descriptions, characters, events, of all that makes a novel great. Once again, like many of the books I have sent you, you might be inclined to think at first, "This story won't speak to me." After all, a story set in Lorain, Ohio, in the early 1940s, mostly told from the point of view of children; a cast of characters who are poor and whose blackness makes them not just a skin colour removed from you and me but a world removed; a perspective that is innately feminist—there is much in this story that starts where you and I have never been.

And yet it will speak to you. Read, read beyond the first few pages, plunge into the story the way you might dive into a chilly lake—and you will find that it's warmer than you expected, that in fact you're quite comfortable in its waters. You will find that the characters—Claudia, Frieda, Pecola—are not so unfamiliar, because you were once a child yourself, and you will find that the cruelty, the racism, the inequality are not so alien either, because we've all experienced the nastiness of the human heart, either in being the one lashed or the one lashing out.

The making of art, as I may have mentioned to you before, involves a lot of work. Because of that, it is implicitly constructive. One doesn't work so hard merely to destroy. One rather hopes to build. No matter how much cruelty and sadness a story may hold, its effect is always the opposite. So a glad tale is taken gladly, and a cruel tale is taken ironically, with feelings of pity and terror, pushing one to reject cruelty. Art then is implicitly liberal; it encourages us towards openness and generosity, it seeks to unlock doors. I suspect this will be the effect of *The Bluest Eye* on you, with its many lives blighted by poverty, stifled by racism, dashed by random cruelty. You will feel more keenly the suffering of others, no matter how different you thought they were from you at first.

Yours truly,
Yann Martel

TONI MORRISON (b. 1931), born Chloe Anthony Wofford, is an American author of novels, short stories, children's literature and nonfiction. Some of her most famous publications include *The Bluest Eye, Song of Solomon* and *Beloved*. She is a member of the American Academy of Arts and Letters and has won multiple awards, including a Pulitzer Prize and, in 1993, the Nobel Prize in Literature. Beyond her career as an author, she has been a literary critic, lecturer, editor, professor and chair at several universities.

BOOK 35

UNDER MILK WOOD
BY DYLAN THOMAS
August 5, 2008

To Stephen Harper,
Prime Minister of Canada,
From a Canadian writer,
With best wishes,
Yann Martel

Dear Mr. Harper,

Your latest book will be late this week. I'm sorry about that. The delay is not due to the long weekend. Like most self-employed workers, I'm willing to work on weekends and during holidays because if I don't do the job, no one will do it for me. The problem lies elsewhere. The book that accompanies this letter, *Under Milk Wood*, by the Welsh poet Dylan Thomas (1914–1953), is such a lyrical work that it demands not only to be read but to be heard. So I thought I'd send you an audio version in addition to the text. There is a famous performance recorded in New York with Dylan Thomas himself reading several of the parts, done hardly two months before his death, and my family owns an LP of that recording, but I'm not willing to part with it, and even if I were, I doubt you have a record player at hand. The more recent performance that I've found for you, on CD, is a BBC production and it's been slow to arrive in the mail. Hence the delay.

A word about audiobooks. Have you ever listened to one? I went on a road trip to the Yukon a few years ago and brought some along to give them a try. I thought I'd dislike having a voice insistently whispering me a story while Canada's majestic northern landscape surged before my eyes. A three-minute pop song I can handle—but a twelve-hour story? I thought it would drive me crazy. I was wrong. Be forewarned: audiobooks are totally addictive. The origin of language is oral, not written. We spoke before we wrote, as children but also as a species. It's in being spoken that words achieve their full power. If the written word is the recipe, then the spoken word is the dish prepared, the voice adding tone, accent, emphasis, emotion. As I'm sure you will agree, the quality of oratory in Canadian and American public life has deteriorated in the last few years. Barack Obama is where he is, on the cusp of the US presidency, in part, I believe, because of his skill in making his words lofty, inspirational and convincing. His ability is unusual. Most public speakers nowadays are plodding. Actors are the great exception. Their public speaking is superb because it is the very basis of their trade. And it's actors who read the stories on audiobooks. The combination of a writer's carefully chosen words and an actor's carefully calibrated delivery makes for a package that is spellbinding. Time and again on my trip to the Yukon I wouldn't get out of the car until a chapter had ended. And then the next morning I couldn't wait to get on with the next. As soon as one story was done, I hastened to start another. Every time I go on a car trip now, I stop by the public library to pick up a selection of audiobooks.

There's talk of an election this fall. That means a lot of travelling for you. I suggest you pack a few audiobooks for those long bus and airplane trips you will have to endure. My only advice is to avoid abridged versions. Otherwise, select as you please. Murder mysteries are particularly effective—as is poetry.

Which brings us back to *Under Milk Wood*. Dylan Thomas is no doubt one of the world's most famous poets. He had a rare quality among modern bards: a persona. His aura as a hard-drinking, hard-living writer—one who died young, to boot; always a boon to one's immortality—has helped his poetry, which is of genuine quality, achieve a cult status. His poems are endlessly anthologized. You've no doubt heard of "Do Not Go Gentle into that Good Night."

Under Milk Wood is a radio play. That might make you think it's a tight, fast-paced affair in which a few distinctive voices are aided by clear sound effects. Not at all. There's no plot to speak of, just a day in the life of a Welsh village named Llareggub. Read that name backwards and you'll get an idea of what Dylan Thomas thought there was to do in Welsh villages. But life is still good, and that's what *Under Milk Wood* is at heart, a celebration of life. With an astounding sixty-nine different voices, it's symphonic in effect. What carries the whole piece, its melody so to speak, is Dylan Thomas's gift for language. His words describe, imitate, bubble, scintillate, run, stop, amuse, surprise, enchant. This is verbal beauty at its purest.

Beauty—the word is much bandied about. But like many words that we use all the time—*good, fair, just,* for example— if we look a little closer, we find that behind the cliché lies a philosophical odyssey that goes as far back as human thinking. Clearly, beauty moves us, motivates us, shames us, shapes us. I won't in this letter even try to define what beauty is. Best to leave you to think on it, or to look it up. If you are serious in your curiosity, you'll find yourself following a strand of Western philosophy that goes as far back as Pythagoras (who associated beauty with symmetry), and of course all of visual art concerns itself in one way or another with beauty. There's much there for the mind that wants to study, a lifetime's worth of material.

I'll limit myself to a much narrower focus, and that is the question of beauty and the prose writer. A writer has many tools to tell a story: characterization, plot and description are some of the obvious ones. Tell a gripping story with full-blooded characters in a convincing setting and you've told a good story. Depending on the writer, one element may prevail more than another. So John Grisham or Stephen King will have much plot to show, with some description, but the characters may be there mainly to serve a narrative purpose. A writer like John Banville, on the other hand (do you know him? Irish, an extraordinary stylist), will tend to be less driven by plot, but will have characters and descriptions that are startling in their richness. And so on. Every writer, depending on his or her strengths and interests, will bring some different ratio of ingredients to the making up of a story.

One notion that is constant in all writers, though, is that of beauty. Every writer, in some way, aspires to literary beauty. That might mean a beautiful plot device, elegant in its simplicity. Or it might mean an ability to paint with words, to create such vivid portraits of people or settings that readers feel that they are "seeing" what the writer is describing. More commonly, the writer of serious ambition aspires to beautiful writing; that is, to writing that by dint of apt vocabulary, happy syntax and pleasing cadence will make the reader marvel. I promise you, if one day you are glad-handing and you end up shaking the hand of a writer and you're at a lost for words, if you say, "You're a beautiful writer," you will please that writer. They will know exactly what you mean, that you're not talking about their shoes or their tie or their complexion, but that you're talking about how they lay their words on the page, and they will glow, they will beam, they will nearly wilt under your praise.

But—there's always a but—one has to be careful about beauty. In all walks of life. In our overly visual society, we tend to be too easily won over by beauty, whether it be in a person, in a product or even in a book. A beautifully written book, like a beautiful person, may not have much to say. The beauty of substance often loses out to the beauty of appearance. A good writer knows that beautiful writing can't substitute for having something to say. The best beauty is that in which beauty of form is held up by beauty of content.

Beauty, in another words, can be a mask hiding a vacuum, hiding falsehood, even hiding ugliness.

No danger here, with *Under Milk Wood*. The lyricism of the language rests solidly on Dylan Thomas's gut knowledge that life is good, however bad it may be at times. It is said that Dylan Thomas wrote *Under Milk Wood* in reaction to the atomic bombing of Hiroshima. I doubt that's factually true. It sounds too conveniently perfect. But opposing a radiant symphonic poem against the darkness of a mass killing of civilians does hark to a spiritual truth: that beauty can be a road back to goodness.

Yours truly,
Yann Martel

DYLAN THOMAS (1914–1953) was a Welsh poet, prose writer and playwright. His poems were characteristically dense, lyrical and exuberant, often reflecting on the themes of unity in the natural world and the cyclical nature of life and death. His most famous works include the short story *A Child's Christmas in Wales* and the poem "Do Not Go Gentle into that Good Night." After World War II, he went to the United States on a series of celebrated reading tours, during one of which, while in New York City, he died of a drinking overdose.

BOOK 36

EVERYTHING THAT RISES MUST CONVERGE
BY FLANNERY O'CONNOR
August 18, 2008

To Stephen Harper,
Prime Minister of Canada,
From a Canadian writer,
With best wishes,
Yann Martel

Dear Mr. Harper,

The work now in your hands is the quintessential used book. The cover looks old, both in style and in condition. A number, a price, has been written directly on the cover: $4.50. Someone put a line of tape along the spine to keep the cover from falling off. There's the dash of a black marker along the bottom of the book, the telltale sign of a used book. The pages inside are yellowed with age along their outside edges. You'll notice a further yellow mark along the left side of the first pages; it looks like the book was accidentally soaked once and a watermark has remained. The book unmistakably shows its venerable age. The edition now yours, a first paperback printing, was published forty-one years ago, in 1967. I was four years old, you were nine. Not bad for an assemblage of flimsy elements: cheap paper and thin cardboard.

The book has lasted this long for two reasons: it is good, and so it has been treated well. Inexpensive in price, it has glowed with value in the eyes of all who owned it, and so they handled it with care. As I mentioned to you in an earlier letter, the used book is economically odd: despite age and lack of rarity, it does not depreciate with age. In fact, it is the contrary: if you take good care of this book, in a few years, because it is a first paperback printing, it will go up in value.

That undiminishing richness is of course due to a paperback's inner wealth, all those little black markings. They inhabit a book the way a soul inhabits a body. Books, like people, can't be reduced to the cost of the materials with which they were made. Books, like people, become unique and precious once you get to know them.

That cultural glory, the used paperback, is perfectly represented here by Flannery O'Connor. Neither new nor aged, but rather enduring, she is the typical glittering treasure to be found in a used bookstore. Imagine: for $4.50 I got you her collection of short stories *Everything That Rises Must Converge*. The discrepancy between price and value is laughably out of whack. What it really says is this: the object you are now holding is of such worth that to give it any price is ridiculous, so here, to emphasize the nonsense of the notion, we'll charge you $4.50.

Flannery O'Connor was American. She was born in 1925 in Georgia and she died there in 1964 of lupus. She was only thirty-nine years old. She was religious, devoutly Catholic to be exact, but her faith was not a set of blinkers. Rather, it charged the world with God's grace and made apparent to her the gap between the sacred and the human. By my reckoning, what O'Connor wrote about, over and over, was the Fall. Her stories are about the ruination of Paradise, about the cost of listening to snakes and reaching for apples. They are moral stories, but there's nothing pat about them. By virtue of good writing, fine dark humour, rich characterization and compelling narrative, they sift through life without reducing it.

And so their effect. Each story feels, has the weight, of a small novel. And with no dull literariness, I assure you. You'll see for yourself. Start on any one of them and a character will quickly reach out from the page, grab you by the arm and pull you along. These stories are engrossing. After each, you will feel that you have lived longer, that you have a greater experience of life, that you are wiser. They are dark stories. In every one, either a son hates his mother or a mother despairs over her useless sons, or it might be a grandfather or a father who is despairing. And the end result, besides highly entertaining, is invariably tragic. Hence the wisdom given off. It's nearly a mathematical equation: reader + story of folly = wiser reader.

I especially recommend to you the stories "Greenleaf," "A View of the Woods" and "The Lame Shall Enter First."

I have another matter I would like to raise with you. The cancellation of PromArt was recently announced. The program, administered by the Department of Foreign Affairs, helps cover some of the travel costs of Canadian artists and cultural groups going abroad to promote their work. The grants to individuals are small, often between $750 and $1500. The budget of the entire program is only $4.7 million. That's about 14 cents a year per Canadian. For that small sum, Canada shows its best, most enduring quality to the nations of the earth. To remind you of what I'm sure you already know, a country cannot be reduced to the corporations it happens to shelter. Businesses come and go, following their own commercial logic. No one feels deep, patriotic feelings for a corporation, certainly not its shareholders. They will vote where the money leads them. So while Canadians can feel proud about such global players as Bombardier and Alcan and hosts of others, we should not pin our identity to them. Canada is a people, not a business. We shine because of our cultural achievements, not our mercantile wealth. So to cut an international arts promotion program is to vow our country to cultural anonymity. It means foreigners will have no impressions of Canada, and so no affection.

The PromArt program is a vital part of our foreign policy. I ask you to reconsider the decision to shut it down. The value-added worth of this modest program is akin to, well, the value-added worth of a paperback.

Yours truly,
Yann Martel

FLANNERY O'CONNOR (1925–1964) was an American essayist, novelist and short story writer whose work is often called grotesque, disturbing and typical of Southern Gothic literature. Her writing is characterized by blunt foreshadowing, irony and allegory, and generally explores questions of religion and morality. Among her best-known works are her novels *Wise Blood* and *The Violent Bear It Away*, and her short story collections *Everything That Rises Must Converge* and *A Good Man Is Hard to Find*. After spending time in New York City and at an artists' colony, she was diagnosed with lupus and returned to her family farm, where she lived for the last fourteen years of her life, raising peacocks and writing. She was posthumously awarded the National Book Award for *The Complete Stories of Flannery O'Connor*.

BOOK 37

A MODEST PROPOSAL
BY JONATHAN SWIFT
September 1, 2008

To Stephen Harper,
Prime Minister of Canada,
A cookbook of sorts,
From a Canadian writer,
With best wishes,
Yann Martel

Dear Mr. Harper,

So, more cuts in arts funding. In my last letter I mentioned only the PromArt program, not having got wind yet of the other cuts. Nearly $45 million in all. That will bite, that will hurt, that will kill. With less art in the future, I wonder what you think there will be more of. What does $45 million buy that has more worth than a people's cultural expression, than a people's sense of who they are?

This calls for a special book. How we administer ourselves—the people we elect, the laws they enact—finds itself reflected in art. Politics is also culture. *A Modest Proposal*, by the Irish writer Jonathan Swift (1667–1745), is a good example of an artistic reflection upon politics. It is a piece of satire, admirable for its humorous ferocity and brevity. At a mere eight pages, it is the shortest work I've ever sent you.

The key paragraph, enunciating Swift's suggested solution to Ireland's poverty, the modest proposal in question, goes like this:

I have been assured by a very knowing American of my acquaintance in London, that a young healthy child well nursed is at a year old a most delicious, nourishing, and wholesome food, whether stewed, roasted, baked or boiled; and I make no doubt that it will equally serve in a fricassee or a ragout.

The question is simple and pertinent, Mr. Harper: are you preparing a ragout?

Yours truly,
Yann Martel

JONATHAN SWIFT (1667–1745) was an Irish satirist and essayist, and a founding member of the Martinus Scriblerus Club, whose members included Alexander Pope and Thomas Parnell. Swift was politically involved, writing pamphlets first for the Whigs, then for the Tories, before championing Irish concerns. He studied in Ireland and England, earning an MA from Oxford, and was an ordained Anglican minister. Swift's style is playful and humorous while being intensely critical of the objects of his satire. His best-known works include *Gulliver's Travels*, *A Modest Proposal* and *The Battle of the Books*.

BOOK 38

ANTHEM

BY AYN RAND

September 15, 2008

To Stephen Harper,

Prime Minister of Canada,

Ayn Rand wanted us to be selfish,

but democracy asks us to be generous.

From a Canadian writer,

With best wishes,

Yann Martel

Dear Mr. Harper,

You've called an election. Appropriate then to send you Ayn (rhymes with Pine) Rand, whose books are highly political. It's very easy to dislike Ayn Rand, not only the writer, but even the person behind the writing, and many readers and intellectuals do indeed dislike her, intensely. However, more than a quarter century after her death (she lived from 1905 to 1982), Ayn Rand still has her dogged followers, a cult nearly, and her books continue to sell in great numbers. There is clearly something both attractive and off-putting about her writing. Her brief novel *Anthem*, just 123 pages, is a useful work to discuss in the context of an election. You will see in what follows that I fall on the side of those who dislike Ayn Rand.

Anthem, first published in 1938, is a dystopia with a utopian heart, a portrayal of a future where everything has gone wrong but where the reader is shown how things can be made right. The novel starts well. The language is simple, the writing understated, the cadence engaging. The story is told entirely from the point of view of the main character, whose name is Equality 7–2521. (Ayn Rand gives her characters names that clearly indicate the notions, the ideals, she wishes to debunk.) Equality 7–2521 does not live in good times. He has no significant freedoms. He has chosen neither where to live nor what to do for a living. He has no family and no real friends. In that, he is like every other man he knows, living a life of rigid conformity that is socially useful but grinding. The reader accepts this premise willingly because of a clever and effective linguistic device on Ayn Rand's part: the complete absence of singular personal pronouns. Equality 7–2521 does not speak as an "I," nor is anything ever his with a "my" or a "mine." Such individualistic concepts are banned from his society and he is a "we," as is everyone else, and all are at the service of the collectivity. As Equality 7–2521 says:

> We strive to be like all our brother men, for all men must be alike. Over the portals of the Palace of the World Council, there are words cut in the marble, which we repeat to ourselves whenever we are tempted:
>
> > "We are one in all and all in one.
> > There are no men but only the great WE,
> > One, indivisible and forever."

Union 5–3992 and International 4–8818, fellow street sweepers, manage to endure such conformity, but:

> There are Fraternity 2–5503, a quiet boy with wise, kind eyes, who cry suddenly, without reason, in the midst of day or night, and their body shakes with sobs they cannot explain.

There are Solidarity 9–6347, who are a bright youth, without fear in the day; but they scream in their sleep, and they scream: "Help us! Help us! Help us!" into the night, in a voice which chills our bones . . .

As for Fraternity 9–3452, Democracy 4–6998, Unanimity 7–3304, International 1–5537, Solidarity 8–1164, Alliance 6–7349, Similarity 5–0306, and especially Collective 0–0009 (they are a nasty one), they are the oppressive system's prime defenders, and they will collide with Equality 7–2521, who is pushed irresistibly to think on his own and pursue his ideas, no matter where they lead him.

There are women. They live separately. Only once a year, for a single night during the "Time of Mating," do men and women come together, in pairs matched by the "Council of Eugenics." It is not then, but earlier, on the City's limits one work day, that Equality 7–2521 meets Liberty 5–3000. He falls in love with her, committing "the great Transgression of Preference." He calls her—they call them—"The Golden One."

This love of his, combined with his independent thinking, eventually forces Equality 7–2521 to flee the City for the Uncharted Forest. The Golden One joins him there. Far from dying in the forest, as he had expected, they find pastoral relief from the oppression of their urban lives. Better yet, they come upon an abandoned house in mountains beyond the forest and they find happiness. They find it because of books left in that house, relics from the ancient times before the "Great Rebirth." Equality 7–2521 begins to read and he comes upon a word, a concept, a philosophy, that gives expression to all the confused mental yearning he has been going through, the word "I."

That discovery—it is revealed on page 108 in the edition I am sending you, fifteen pages before the end of the book, the very beginning of Chapter 11, starting with the words "I am. I think. I will"—is where *Anthem* goes to pot. The point of Ayn Rand's fiction, as I'm sure you will have seized, is a critique of collectivism, typified at its most terrible by the horrors of communism under Stalin in Russia, the country of Rand's birth (she became an American citizen in 1931). And there, the reader, certainly this reader, is with her. Bloodthirsty dictatorships are repulsive to every sane human being. But Ayn Rand makes two mistakes in her allegory of life in the Soviet Union. First, she sees only the worst in collectivism, throwing out wholesale the good with the bad. To her, the Gulag and socialized health care, for example, were instances of one and the same evil. Second, in rejecting Stalin and his damnable system, she goes to an absurd opposite libertarian extreme. Rand posited that humanity would be happiest if we lived as autarkic individuals, beholden to no one, unbounded, unfettered, free, free, free. The virtue of selfishness, that's what Ayn Rand is all about. It's even the title of one of her books. No wonder Rand appeals mostly to two disparate groups of readers: adolescents in the throes of carving out their individuality, and right-wing American capitalists bent on making and keeping too much money.

Back to the novel. Equality 7–2521, on page 108, has bust free thanks to the word "I." What follows is an orgy of I-ism, of me, me, me, mine, mine, mine:

> My hands . . . My spirit . . . My sky . . . My forest . . . This earth of mine . . .

You know you're in trouble when someone claims to own the sky. As much as Equality 7–2521 was appealing when he was oppressed, once he is free he becomes annoying, pretentious, repelling. While his strange speech in the City—we this, we that—came off as noble and incantatory, his free speech in the mountains is dull and pompous. The struggling hero whom we cheered on has become just another self-righteous, domineering male who thinks he knows everything. We sympathized with his plight, but now we shudder at his solution:

> I wished to know the meaning of things. I am the meaning. . . . Whatever road I take, the guiding star is within me; the guiding star and the loadstone which point the way. They point in but one direction. They point to me. . . . I owe nothing to my brothers, nor do I gather debts from them. I ask none to live for me, nor do I live for any others. . . . And now I see the face of god, and I raise this god over the earth, this god whom men have sought since men came into being, this god who will grant them joy and peace and pride.
>
> This god, this one word:
> "I."

You are a religious man, Mr. Harper. You will know that the essence of every religion, of every god, is precisely the opposite of what Ayn Rand is speechifying about: God is about the abandonment of the self, not its exaltation. But that is an aside, a minor point. The main problem with Rand's libertarianism, this über-Nietzschean cult of the heroic individual standing on a mountaintop, is that it makes not only society unworkable, but even simple relations. An example jumps out in Rand's own novel. Equality 7–2521, now drunk with his own uniqueness, has naturally tired of his name. He says to the Golden One:

> "I have read of a man who lived many thousands of years ago, and of all the names in these books, his is the one I wish to

bear. He took the light of the gods and he brought it to men, and he taught men to be gods. And he suffered for his deed as all bearers of light must suffer. His name was Prometheus."

Prometheus, the nice guy formerly known as Equality 7–2521, goes on:

"And I have read of a goddess who was the mother of the earth and of all the gods. Her name was Gaea. Let this be your name, my Golden One, for you are to be the mother of a new kind of gods."

What if the Golden One rather fancied herself as a Lynette or a Bobbie-Jean? Who is this Prometheus to tell her what her name should be? And what if she doesn't want to be the mother of a screaming gaggle of kids? What if one child will do, and a girl if possible, thank you very much?

But, headstrong as Liberty 5–3000 seemed to be in the City, as Gaea she is passive and submissive, doing as she is told, because nothing and no one should get in the way of Ayn Rand's romantic Superman, especially not his woman.

And what does Prometheus intend to do with his new-found freedom? He'll raid the City for "chosen friends" and conquer the world!

Here, on this mountain, I and my sons and my chosen friends shall build our new land and our fort. . . . And the day will come when I shall break all the chains of the earth, and raze the cities of the enslaved, and my home will become the capital of a world where each man will be free to exist for his own sake.

Well, what does he want, does he want to be free and unfettered or a bustling capital?

The novel ends, with trumpeting triumphalism, as follows:

And here, over the portals of my fort, I shall cut in the stone the word which is to be my beacon and my banner. . . . The word which can never die on this earth, for it is the heart of it and the meaning and the glory.

The sacred word:

EGO

Just the kind of neighbour we all want, the loud, overbearing oaf with the poor, mousy wife who has the word EGO carved over his door.

That is the paradox and failure of Ayn Rand's vision. Her response to the excesses of collectivism is an excessive and simplistic egoism. The more realistic challenge in life is to be oneself amidst others, to heed one's own needs and at the same time satisfy the demands of one's community. It is not easy. Life, and not only politics, is the art of compromise.

That push and pull between the needs of the individual and the needs of the collectivity is at the heart of an election. If every voter votes strictly according to self-interest, then the collectivity, the nation, will be riven by discord and divisions and will risk falling apart. But if the collective We is overfed, then its constituent elements are starved. Every politician, and you first and foremost, Mr. Harper, must balance personal interest with what is good for the nation. If you divide and conquer too much, if you heed too little, then the country will suffer, as will your reputation in history. Enlightened statesmanship is required by all, both voters and politicians. But that's a risky sell, isn't it, trying to peddle a better future to voters worried about their immediate present? The best is demanded of all of us. I can only hope we will get it.

Since we have an election on our hands, let me make my personal appeal. Don't worry, it won't cost anything. I won't bay about arts funding or the centrality of art in our lives or even, more cravenly, about the profitability of the arts industry in Canada (what was the sum I read recently, $47 billion in 2007 alone, more than the profits from the mining industry? Not that I buy that argument. The essential is inherently profitable, existentially. The individual who is artless is poor, no matter how much money he or she may have). No, I only want to give you for free an idea, the following:

What if a reading list were established for prospective prime ministers of Canada, to ensure that they have sufficient imaginative depth to be at the helm of our country? After all, we expect a prime minister to have a fair knowledge of the history and geography of Canada, to know something about economics and public administration, about current events and foreign affairs, the financial assets of a prime minister are accountable to us, so why shouldn't his or her imaginative assets also be accountable?

Because that has been the whole point of our literary duet, hasn't it? If you haven't read, now or earlier, any of the books I have suggested, or books like them, if you haven't read *The Death of Ivan Ilych* or any other Russian novel, if you haven't read *Miss Julia* or any other Scandinavian play, if you haven't read *Metamorphosis* or any other German-language novel, if you haven't read *Waiting for Godot* or *To the Lighthouse* or any other experimental play or novel, if you haven't read *Artists and Models* or any other erotica, if you haven't read the *Meditations* of Marcus Aurelius or *The Educated Imagination* or any other philosophical inquiry, if you haven't read *Under Milk Wood* or any other poetic prose, if you haven't read *Their Eyes Were Watching God* or *Drown* or any other American novel, if you haven't read *The Cellist of Sarajevo* or *The Island Means Minago* or *The Dragonfly of Chicoutimi* or any other Canadian novel, poem or play—then what is your mind made of? What materials went into the building of the dreams you have for our country? What is the colour, the pattern, the rhyme and reason of your imagination? These are not questions one is usually entitled to ask, but once someone has power over me, then, yes, I do have the right to probe your imagination, because your dreams may become my nightmares.

This Prime Minister's Reading List could be administered by the Speaker of the House of Commons, an impartial figure, perhaps benefiting from recommendations not only from Members of Parliament but from all Canadian citizens. It would be a hard list to set up, that's for sure. How to represent concisely all that the written word has done, here and abroad, in English and French and other languages? The Prime Minister's Reading List couldn't be too long; we wouldn't want you sitting around reading novels your whole mandate. And it would be subject to regular updates, of course, to reflect changing times and tastes. How to implement the list would be another challenge. Would it be a yearly reading list, or just one at the beginning of each term? And how to check that you've actually read the books and not had an assistant summarize them for you? Would you have to write an exam, pen an essay, face a committee, answer questions during a Question Period exclusively devoted to the matter?

"I have no time for this nonsense," you might feel like shouting. But as I said to you in my very first letter, there is a space next to every bed where a book can be lying in wait. And I ask you again: what is your mind made of?

So, would that be an idea, to set up a Prime Minister's Reading List? What is your position on this vital issue?

I await your answer.

Yours truly,
Yann Martel

AYN RAND (1905–1982) was a Russian-born American novelist, playwright and screenwriter. Her most famous novels are *The Fountainhead* and *Atlas Shrugged*. Within two weeks of arriving in Hollywood to launch her screenwriting career, Rand was hired as an extra and then a script reader for director Cecil B. DeMille, and met her future husband, the actor Frank O'Connor, to whom she would stay married for fifty years. She was also politically active. Her works prominently reflect a belief in individualism, capitalism and basic civil liberties, as well as her staunch opposition to collectivist political structures.

BOOK 39

MISTER PIP
BY LLOYD JONES
September 29, 2008

To Stephen Harper,
Prime Minister of Canada,
Words take you places.
Best wishes,
Lloyd Jones
September 21
Brisbane, Australia.

Sent to you by
a Canadian writer,
With best wishes,
Yann Martel

Dear Mr. Harper,

Campaigning must be gruelling, especially when you are head
of a party. You work and travel constantly, you speak to people
morning, noon and evening, you must always be on your guard,
and all of it is very personal. The worst, I imagine, is the complete loss of privacy. Any time you might want for yourself
must be sacrificed to the demands of public life.

An excellent way to climb back into yourself is to read a
book. I suspect that reading is such a satisfying experience
because it is at one and the same time a dialogue —between
your mind and an external source of words—and an entirely

private experience. When you are reading, your guard needn't be up. You can be entirely yourself. Even better: you are totally free. You can read slowly or quickly, you can reread a section or skip it, why, you can even throw the book down and pick up another—it's all up to you. The freedom goes even further: what you experience while reading is also entirely your own affair. You can let yourself be engrossed by what you are reading, or you can let your mind wander. You can be a receptive reader, or, if you want, an obstreperous one. The freedom, I repeat, is total. When else do we have such a feeling? Is it not the case that in most every other activity, personal or social, we are hemmed in by rules and regulations, by the intrusions and expectations of others?

Reading is one of the best ways to bring on that essential condition for the thinking person, one that I mentioned at the start of our exchange: stillness. All the noise and confusion of the outer world falls away, is blocked off, when one is reading and one becomes still. Which is to say, one enters into dialogue with oneself, asking questions, coming up with replies, feeling and assessing facts and emotions. That is why reading is so fortifying, because in setting us free it allows us to re-centre ourselves, it allows the mind's eye to look at itself in a mirror and take stock.

What better book to bear witness to this process than *Mister Pip,* by the New Zealand writer Lloyd Jones. Your mind will travel far with this novel. For starters, the story takes place on the Pacific island of Bougainville, part of Papua New Guinea. But it also takes place, in a way, in Victorian England. There's a quieting appeal right there, isn't there? Who hasn't dreamed of spending time on an island in the Pacific, surrounded by blue sea and tropical greenery? And who doesn't like visiting Europe?

Mister Pip is a novel about a novel. The name Pip might be familiar to you. It's the name of the main character in *Great*

Expectations, the novel by Charles Dickens. This is no coincidence. *Great Expectations* is a character in Jones's novel, one might say. It is certainly the catalyst to much of the action in it.

On Bougainville, a white man, Mr. Watts, lives in a village of black people who accept him because he is married to one of them, Grace, who has gone crazy, but of whom Mr. Watts takes loving care. A rebellion shuts down the local mine and results in the evacuation of all the whites who work there. Only Mr. Watts stays on. He and the villagers are cut off from the rest of the world by a blockade. Mr. Watts agrees to become the schoolteacher. But he knows precious little. Chemistry is just a word, and history little more than a list of famous names. One thing he does know and love, though, is Charles Dickens's great novel. He reads it to the children. They are enchanted. They fall in love with Pip. But their parents and even more so the government troops that routinely descend upon the village to terrorize its inhabitants are suspicious of this Mr. Pip. Where is he hiding? Produce him or else, they warn.

Lloyd Jones's novel is about how literature can create a new world. It is about how the world can be read like a novel, and a novel like the world. If that sounds twee, be warned that there is also shocking meanness and violence in *Mister Pip*.

Does the violence make the fable-like element pale in comparison? Does "reality" come through and displace the "fiction"? Not at all. You will see. The novel argues that the imagination, whether religious or artistic, is what makes the world bearable.

I am also sending you *Great Expectations*. It's not necessary to have read it to understand *Mister Pip*, but it is such an enjoyable masterpiece that I thought I'd throw it in as an extra pleasure.

I had the pleasure of meeting Lloyd Jones just last week at the Brisbane Literary Festival. He kindly agreed to autograph your copy of his novel.

May you enjoy both *Mister Pip* and *Great Expectations*. Better still: may they bring you stillness.

Yours truly,
Yann Martel

LLOYD JONES (b. 1955) is a New Zealander who has been publishing books since 1985. His experiences as a journalist and travel writer have imbued his novels with a strong sense of realism. His most recent novel, *Mister Pip*, won the Commonwealth Writers' Prize for Best Book in 2007. Other well-known works by Jones include *Biografi, Here at the End of the World We Learn to Dance, Paint Your Wife* and *The Book of Fame*. Several of his novels have been successfully adapted for the stage. Jones has also written books for children, and edited an anthology of sports writing.

BOOK 40

A CLOCKWORK ORANGE
BY ANTHONY BURGESS
October 13, 2008

To Stephen Harper,
Prime Minister of Canada,
"What's it going to be then, eh?"
From a Canadian writer,
With best wishes,
Yann Martel

Dear Mr. Harper,

Meet Alex. He's the nightmare of both citizens and governments, the first because they are afraid of him and the second because they don't know what to do with him. Alex, you see, is a-lex, outside the law, from the Latin. He and his friends mug people, loot stores and invade homes, liberally dishing out extreme violence and routinely indulging in gang rape. And to think he's only fifteen. When he's caught, he rots in a juvenile home for a while until he's let out—and then what? Well, why stop when you're having such a good time? He gets back to the fun of "ultra-violence." Welcome to the world of *A Clockwork Orange,* a brilliant short novel by the English writer Anthony Burgess (1917–1993), published in 1962.

"What's it going to be then, eh?" That slightly bullying question appears at the beginning of each of the novel's three sections. It is asked not only of one or another of the story's characters; it is asked of us. What's it going to be with Alex then, eh? What are we to do with him? *A Clockwork Orange*, despite the great violence in it, in fact, because of it, is a morally preoccupied work.

When Alex is caught after his latest bout of thuggish mayhem, the authorities try a different approach. They try conditioning. If a dog can be conditioned to salivate upon hearing a bell tinkling, why can't a boy be conditioned to reject violence? Alex is subjected to the Ludovico Method, in which he is given injections that make him feel deathly nauseous at the same time as he is being shown extremely violent films. He thus learns to become sickened by violence, literally. Unfortunately, because of the soundtrack of some of the reels he is forced to watch, Alex is also accidentally conditioned to feel revulsion upon hearing classical music. This aggrieves him greatly because our Alex, despite his brutal tendencies, is a music lover (sounds historically familiar, doesn't it?).

A minor matter, the Minister of the Interior feels. Our main problem is solved. Now, when our boy sees violence, when he merely entertains thoughts of violence, he falls over helplessly, clutching his stomach and retching. If he also keels over when he hears Beethoven, so what? That's just a little collateral damage.

But if goodness is elected not by free choice but as a self-defence mechanism against nausea, is it morally valid goodness? "Is a man who chooses the bad perhaps in some way better than a man who has the good imposed on him?" the prison chaplain asks at one point. Burgess's answer is unequivocal: he chooses goodness as a free choice. And the reason why this answer is correct is given in the novel's key words, coming from Alex, dropped nearly casually in the middle of a long sentence:

I was still puzzling out all this and wondering whether I should refuse to be strapped down to this chair tomorrow and start a real bit of dratsing with them all, because I had my rights, when another chelloveck came in to see me.

I had my rights. Indeed, Alex does have his rights, as we all do. Ignore those rights, and the essential is lost: "When a man cannot choose he ceases to be a man."

A group of intellectuals opposed to the government decides to make use of Alex. They lock him in a room next to which they play loud classical music. Alex takes the only exit they've left him, an open window. The room is in an apartment block, several floors up. Alex plummets to the sidewalk—and straight into the hearts of citizens indignant at the brainwashing he's been subjected to. An election is in the offing and the Government is nervous about its prospects. At the hospital where he is recovering from his serious injuries, Alex's conditioning is hastily reversed. Alex is very happy about this. In the last scene of the penultimate chapter of the novel, we find him lying back, listening with renewed delight to Beethoven's Ninth. "I was cured all right," he says.

That line, if it were the last line of the book, would be fiercely ironic. Good that the boy's ears have been restored, but so has his moral compass. Its fine, trembling needle can now, once again, point as freely towards good as it can towards bad. Does that mean we citizens should start to tremble too? No worries, says Burgess in the last chapter of the book, Chapter 21. Alex's ordeal has eaten up over two years of his life. He's now eighteen and has matured. The joys of rape and pillage just aren't what they used to be. Alex is now more in the mood to find himself a nice girl, settle down and start a family. The novel ends with a softer, mellower Alex pining for a mate.

A weak ending, I'd say. Burgess successfully makes the case for the imperative of freedom at the level of the individual when making moral choices. But what are we to do at the level of a society? What choices does a society have in the face of citizens who are a-lex? Each of us must be free to be fully ourselves, granted, but how should a society balance the freedom of the individual with the safety of the group? Burgess avoids this difficult question by having Alex suddenly discover the peaceable joys of family life. To a social problem Burgess gives only an unpredictable individual solution. What if Alex had decided to continue with his life of violence?

The American edition of *A Clockwork Orange* was originally published without the last chapter. This editorial cut, which Burgess opposed, does throw the construction of the novel off balance. Nonetheless, Alex's uncertain claim at the end of Chapter 20 that he is cured is, I think, an ending more consistent with the material that has come earlier. It is this truncated version that Stanley Kubrick used to make his celebrated movie. He too clearly preferred a conclusion that wasn't so facilely optimistic.

What I've said so far may make you think that *A Clockwork Orange* is a blandly pious work, reducible to a few moral bromides. That's not the case. Just as a hockey game can't be reduced to its score, so a work of art can't be reduced to a summary. What makes *A Clockwork Orange* incompressible is its language. Alex and his friends speak a most peculiar English. Here's a sample, taken at random:

> I did not quite kopat what he was getting at govoreeting about calculations, seeing that getting better from feeling bolnoy is like your own affair and nothing to do with calculations. He sat down, all nice and droogy, on the bed's edge . . .

A mixture of English slang and words derived from Russian, delivered in cadences that sometimes sound Biblical, at other times Elizabethan, it is this language, Nadsat, that makes *A Clockwork Orange* an enduring work of literature. It is the juice in the orange. The context makes the meaning of most Nadsat words clear, and the occasional befuddlement is not unpleasant.

Canadians go to the polls tomorrow. I offer you *A Clockwork Orange* the day before for a good reason. There's an element in the novel that is eerily familiar. The government under which Alex lives is democratically elected, yet it has recourse to policies that undermine the foundations of democracy. We have seen these kinds of policies for eight years now in the United States, a country morally bankrupted by its current president. You claim to have a solution for what to do with Alex. The experts disagree with you, as do the courts and the people; certainly the people in Quebec are resisting your ideas. But you think you know better.

Are you sure, Mr. Harper, that what you have up your sleeve aren't so many Ludovico Methods?

Yours truly,
Yann Martel

P.S. Have you seen Kubrick's classic adaptation? It's one of those rare cases where the movie is as good as the book. I'll try to find a DVD copy. When I do, I'll send it along.

ANTHONY BURGESS (1917–1993) was a prolific English novelist, poet, playwright, biographer, literary critic, linguist, translator and composer. His publications run the gamut from linguistically sophisticated literary novels like his Malayan trilogy, *The Long Day Wanes*, to criticism of works by James Joyce, to symphonies, to dystopian satires.

BOOK 41

GILGAMESH
IN AN ENGLISH VERSION BY STEPHEN MITCHELL

October 27, 2008

To Stephen Harper,
Prime Minister of Canada,
The oldest story in the world, to celebrate your second minority,
From a Canadian writer,
With best wishes,
Yann Martel

Dear Mr. Harper,

Congratulations on your electoral win. You must be pleased with your increased minority. What your continued tenure as prime minister means, among other things, is that our book club has survived. We can now really settle into this business of discussing books. Since we have more time, why don't we go back in time. Why don't we start where book talk probably started, along the banks of the river Euphrates. What has become known as the standard version of the epic of *Gilgamesh* was set down between the years 1300 and 1000 BCE in cuneiform on twelve clay tablets in Babylonian, a dialect of the Akkadian language. But earlier written fragments in Sumerian about the heartbroken king of Uruk date from around 2000 BCE, and the historical Gilgamesh, well, he died in about 2750 BCE, just a couple of centuries shy of five thousand years ago.

Gilgamesh predates Homer and predates the Bible. It is the cultural soil out of which these later texts emerged, which is why some elements in the epic will sound familiar to you. Before the biblical Flood there was the Great Flood in *Gilgamesh*. Before Noah's Ark, there was the ship Utnapishtim built, crowded with animals. In *Gilgamesh*, there is an odyssey before the *Odyssey* and there is one who overcame mortality before Jesus of Nazareth overcame it. The theme of a terrible flood also finds itself echoed in the Hindu story of Matsya the fish, Vishnu's first avatar, and the theme of fear will perhaps remind you of the *Bhagavad Gita*, which I sent you last year. Remember Arjuna's fear before the battle? It is not dissimilar to Gilgamesh's fear before death. The inexorableness of fate might remind you of classical Greek thinking, just as the petulance of the Sumerian gods is much like that of the Greek gods. *Gilgamesh* is the mother of all stories. We, as literary animals, start with *Gilgamesh*.

That might make you think that reading the epic will be like staring into a display window of crude stone sculptures in an archaeology museum. Not so, I promise you, certainly not in the version of *Gilgamesh* that I'm sending you, by the American translator Stephen Mitchell. He's done away with scholarly encrustations and dull fidelity to disjointed fragments (though, if you care, there is a good introduction and lots of notes). Mitchell has sought to be faithful to the spirit of the original, more mindful of the needs of the English reader than the sensibility of the archaeologist.

The result is exhilarating. The prose is simple, vigorous and stately, the action thrillingly dramatic. I encourage you to read the epic aloud. It's an easy oral read, you will see. Your tongue will not trip, your mind will not stumble. Like the beating of a drum, the cadence of the beats and the repetition of some passages will hold you in thrall.

The mind can be immortal, living forever through ideas. An idea can leap from mind to mind, going down through the generations, forever keeping ahead of death. The mind of Plato, for example, is still with us, long dead though he is. But the heart? The heart is inescapably mortal. Every heart dies. Of Plato's heart, its share of things felt, we know nothing. *Gilgamesh* is the story of one man's heart and its breaking in the face of death. The emotional immediacy is palpable. Gilgamesh, king of great-walled Uruk, won't seem alien to you because that aggrieved voice pleading directly in your ear isn't from over four thousand years ago—it's the pulsing of your own perishable heart. Our only hope is that we might live as authentically as Gilgamesh and find a friend as loving and loyal as Enkidu.

There are some lovely lines. Keep an eye out for "A gust of wind passed," and "A gentle rain fell onto the mountains." They glow within their context. And there is a snake that does Gilgamesh a bad turn. That too will be biblically familiar to you. This snake, though, does not proffer; it takes. But the result is the same: unhappy Gilgamesh must accept his fate as a mortal.

Yours truly,
Yann Martel

STEPHEN MITCHELL (b. 1943) is a polyglot American translator known for his poetic, rather than literal, translations. He has translated works originally written in German, Hebrew, Greek, Latin, French, Spanish, Italian, Chinese, Sanskrit and Danish. His other translations include the Hindu text the *Bhagavad Gita* and the Buddhist *Tao Te Ching*. He has also published a collection of poetry, two novels, three works of non-fiction and several children's books.

BOOK 42

GILGAMESH

IN AN ENGLISH VERSION BY DERREK HINES

November 10, 2008

To Stephen Harper,
Prime Minister of Canada,
Again, but made modern,
From a Canadian writer,
With best wishes,
Yann Martel

Dear Mr. Harper,

Gilgamesh again. But a very different *Gilgamesh*. The version
I sent you two weeks ago took liberties, but the better to serve
the original Sumerian classic. One senses that Stephen Mitchell
took the broken clay tablets, fitted the pieces together and then
adeptly filled in where the cracks made it hard to read. Our
guide on that breathless trip across five thousand years to the
banks of the Euphrates remained egoless and anonymous. Of
Mitchell, we sensed nothing; in fact, we didn't even think to
enquire about him.

With *Gilgamesh* as interpreted by the Canadian poet Derrek
Hines, the time travel is in the opposite direction. It's
Mesopotamia that's yanked into the present day, every speck of
archaeological dust blown off. This version is all about liberties, and the clay tablets have been thrown out. Take the opening
lines. In the Mitchell version, they go:

> Surpassing all kings, powerful and tall
> beyond all others, violent, splendid,
> a wild bull of a man, unvanquished leader,
> hero in the front lines, beloved by his soldiers—
> *fortress* they called him, *protector of the people,*
> *raging flood that destroys all defences—*
> two-thirds divine and one-third human . . .

With Hines, we get:

> Here is Gilgamesh, king of Uruk:
> two-thirds divine, a mummy's boy,
> zeppelin ego, cock like a trip-hammer,
> and solid chrome, no-prisoners arrogance.

Get the picture? You don't want to read the versions in the wrong order. With the Mitchell, the scope, the vastness, the timelessness of an ancient epic is felt. With the Hines, you might wonder where the epic went. What's all this *riffing?* Well, that's it, the riffing is the point. Remember Ishtar's anger when Gilgamesh rejects her, how she goes to her father, the god Anu, wanting to borrow the Bull of Heaven so that she can unleash it on Uruk? This is what Hines makes of it, Ishtar speaking:

> "I'll have the Bull of Heaven or I'll unzip Hell,
> and free the un-dead to suck frost into the living."
> Then, on a pulse, an actor's mood change—
> she, pouting: "Darling Anu,
> you know how I'm insulted;
> I want, *want* the Bull of Heaven
> to revenge my honour."

She lifts a perfect foot to stamp,
and the tiles of Heaven's floor in rivalry
shift like a Rubik's cube to receive it.

It's *Gilgamesh* meets Naomi Campbell. Besides the Rubik's cube, there are a great many other un-Mesopotamian references in the text: atomic blasts, Brueghel, buildings in New York, CAT scans, event horizons, express trains, Marlene Dietrich, oxygen masks, paparazzi, Swiss bank accounts, X-rays, the Wizard of Oz, and so on. This joy in the anachronistic bears witness to the very different approach that Hines takes.

All things are met and understood through one mind, the one we have. Timelessness, transcendence, the evanescence of the ego—these are true, but they are not what we experience. They were neither felt by Gilgamesh, nor are they felt by us. We are not all one. We are just one, each on our own. You, me, him, her, six billion times over. Each one of us has a blip note of mortality. It's only when the blips are put together that we seem to hear a symphony throbbing down through time. Mitchell's version of *Gilgamesh* plays on that symphony. He makes the epic new, but it works because we know it's old. Hines wants none of this hand-me-down worth. He's a modern; this blip here and now will speak freshly for that old, fifty-century-old blip. With Hines you get the singularity of the living poet expressing himself in his own right, drawing attention to himself, saying "This is me, this is our language, this is our condition—whaddya think?"

I think it's very good. A harder read than the Mitchell, for sure. At times, the poetic pithiness requires work to unpack. Then in the next stanza, a startling image makes perfect sense. Which is why I would recommend that you read the Hines more than once. It's only sixty pages, and well spaced at that. The more familiar you are with it, the more it will make sense, and soon enough you will have furnished a beautiful room in your mind. It's a rich, exciting text, with some stabbingly brilliant lines. Take this, part of Gilgamesh's lament upon Enkidu's death:

> The complaisant dead inch away,
> dislocating the shared vanishing point
> of our perspective,
> and we struggle to repaint the picture.

A last example. Gilgamesh, after getting "snake-drunk" and losing the herb of eternal life, returns to Uruk to die. He has this to say:

> We are made and broken on a miracle
> we look on and cannot see—as though
> we had sold out instinct to thought
> blinding us to what the world is,
> the heart's gate to eternity.

That is a truth very old and, here, totally modern.

Yours truly,
Yann Martel

DERREK HINES is an award-winning Canadian poet best known for his reinterpretation of the epic *Gilgamesh*. By injecting modern images into his free verse retelling, Hines shrinks the gap of time between Sumerian origins and a contemporary audience, and recharges the tale's powerful effect. Hines has published two books of poetry. Raised in Southern Ontario, he now lives on the Lizard peninsula in Cornwall.

BOOK 43

THE UNCOMMON READER
BY ALAN BENNETT
November 24, 2008

To Stephen Harper,
Prime Minister of Canada,
A short novel on a healthy addiction,
From a Canadian writer,
With best wishes,
Yann Martel

Dear Mr. Harper,

I can't think of a more delightful introduction to the republic of letters than Alan Bennett's short novel *The Uncommon Reader*. One day at the bottom of the Palace garden, parked next to the kitchen garbage bins, alerted by her corgis, the Queen discovers the City of Westminster's travelling library. She pops in to apologize for the barking dogs and, once there, impelled by a sense of duty rather than any real interest, she takes out a book. This simple act marks the beginning of Her Majesty's downfall, in a way. The irony in the story is as light as whipped cream, the humour as appealing as candy, the characterization as crisp as potato chips, but at the heart of it there's something highly nutritious to be digested: the effect that books can have on a life.

Upon finishing the book, you will think you know HM better, you will feel closer to her, you will like her. This is in part because of Bennett's skill in bringing his royal character to life. But it also has to do with the nature of books. In the republic of letters, all readers are equal. Unlike other retail outlets, bookstores don't really come in categories, be it luxury or low-end. A bookstore is a bookstore. Some specialize, but the restriction there has only to do with kinds of books—say modern languages or art—and not with classes of readers. Everyone is welcome in bookstores and all types rub shoulders in them, the wealthy and the poor, the highly educated and the self-taught, the old and the young, the adventurous and the conventional, and others still. You might even bump into the Queen.

Before I forget, one of our very own great Canadian writers, Alice Munro, makes a cameo appearance in *The Uncommon Reader*, on page 67.

Since I'm on the topic of bookstores, I thought I'd include a few snapshots of some that I've visited recently.

The Bookseller Crow on the Hill is in Crystal Palace, a

neighbourhood in the south of London where I've been staying recently. I'm standing next to John, the genial owner, and I'm holding in my hand the very book you now own, which I bought from John. The Crow is not a very big place in terms of square footage, but stand in front on any shelf—New Titles, Fiction, History, Philosophy, Poetry, Travel—and the mental space represented is as vast as the universe.

The next photo is of a small, venerable used bookstore on Milton Street in Montreal called The Word. It has served generations of students. I popped in to buy a novel by the English writer Ivy Compton-Burnett, whom Bennett mentions in his book and whom I'd never read. I found *A Family and a Fortune,* published in 1939. It cost me $3.95.

The last photo is of La Librairie du Square, a French bookstore also in Montreal. It was my father who taped the red poster you see on the glass door. It announces an event organized by PEN, Amnesty International and l'UNEQ to do with freedom of expression and imprisoned writers.

Independent bookstores are a vanishing breed, especially in North America. The ones who suffer the most from this disappearance are not necessarily readers, but neighbourhoods. After all, a large Chapters or Indigo or Barnes & Noble will hold more books than any reader could possibly read in a lifetime. But large chain stores tend to be fewer in number and are often accessible only by car. The Bookseller Crow, on the other hand, is in a row of small stores that includes a clothes stores, a café, a pet store that specializes in fish, a shoe store, a real estate agent, a hairdresser, a newsagent, a bakery, a betting agency, a number of restaurants, and so on. The Word and La Librairie du Square are on streets along which thousands of people walk every day. Whenever an independent bookstore disappears, shareholders somewhere may be richer, but a neighbourhood is for sure poorer.

I'm sorry for writing such a busy letter, but there's one last matter I'd like to mention. A few weeks ago, on October 20 to be exact, I came upon an article in the *New York Times* on a man in Colombia who for the last decade has been travelling around his war-ravaged corner of the country with two donkeys—named Alfa and Beto—loaded with books. He stops in every remote pueblo to read to children and to lend books out. He started his Biblioburro, as he calls it, after seeing the positive effect that reading had on students growing up in a violent and uncertain environment. Ten years on, Luis Soriano remarks that his enterprise has become an obligation, and it is now considered an institution.

The City of Westminster's travelling library and the Biblioburro, the Bookseller Crow on the Hill and The Word—the rich life of the mind that these institutions offer makes joyful equals of us all, from monarchs to poor peasant children.

Yours truly,
Yann Martel

ALAN BENNETT (b. 1934) is an English author, actor, humorist and playwright. His first great success was co-authoring and starring in the comedy revue *Beyond the Fringe*. He then performed in innumerable stage, radio and television productions and wrote several short stories, novellas, non-fiction works and plays. Among his many acclaimed creations are the Academy Award–winning film adaptation *The Madness of King George*, and *The History Boys*, a play that won three Laurence Olivier Awards and was adapted for the screen.

BOOK 44

THE GOOD EARTH
BY PEARL S. BUCK
December 8, 2008

To Stephen Harper,
Prime Minister of Canada,
A novel of fortunes made and lost,
From a Canadian writer,
With best wishes,
Yann Martel

Dear Mr. Harper,

One of the curious aspects of the life and work of Pearl Buck is the speed with which she rose to fame and then sank into comparative obscurity. Her first book was published in 1930. Eight years later, at the remarkably young age of forty-six, she was awarded the Nobel Prize in Literature, only the third American so rewarded, and this, principally on the basis of the three novels that form the trilogy *The House of Earth: The Good Earth* (1931), for which she won the Pulitzer Prize, *Sons* (1932) and *A House Divided* (1935). It is *The Good Earth* I am offering you this week.

Yet after this stellar start, despite continuing to produce quantities of books and fighting for many a good cause, Buck faded from the forefront of literature so that when she died in 1973 she was nearly a forgotten figure. The reasons for this are, I think, easy enough to discern. She wrote too many books—over eighty—and while a very able writer, she was no great experimenter. She didn't renew the novel or its language the way Faulkner and Hemingway did, fellow Americans who are still widely read and studied. Nor can her books—or at least the ones I'm familiar with—be stamped with the label "universal," which sometimes helps an author gain literary immortality. No, the books that made her name were remarkably local, even rooted. Pearl Buck was one of the first writers to bring to life for Western readers that country-civilization called China. It's a country she knew well for having spent a good part of her life there as the daughter of Christian missionaries and then as a missionary and teacher herself. Despite the hardships she endured there at times, China was a country she loved. She saw its people as just that, people, and she observed them with great sympathy and mixed with them and, eventually, wrote about them. She was the writer-as-bridge, and many people chose to cross the bridge she built.

You will see why when you read *The Good Earth*. From the first line—"It was Wang Lung's marriage day"—you slip into the skin of a Chinese peasant from pre-Communist times and you begin to live his life as he sees it and feels it. It's a harsh story, blighted by poverty and famine, and harsher still for the women in it, but it's also entirely engrossing. *The Good Earth* is the sort of novel you'll be itching to get back to whenever you have to put it down. After reading it, you'll feel that you know what it might mean to be Chinese at a certain time and in a certain part of China. Therein lies the passing nature of Buck's work. China has changed radically since *The Good Earth* was published. What was new and revelatory then is now hoary and out of date. The main appeal of Buck's work today is in the power of her stories rather than their currency.

Still, *The Good Earth* remains an excellent introduction to old China and a vivid parable on the fragility of fortune, how things gained can be lost, how what is built can easily be destroyed. This lesson will not be lost on you considering the political turmoil you are now going through. The fate of a politician is so terribly uncertain. Pearl Buck is a staple of every used bookstore. She is still widely read. Her name evokes fond memories. Whereas politicians, when they go, when they disappear from the stage, kicking and screaming sometimes, they really go, they vanish into oblivion so that quickly people scratch their heads, trying to remember when exactly they were in power and what they accomplished.

Yours truly,
Yann Martel

PEARL S. BUCK (1892–1973) was a Pulitzer Prize–winning American author and the first American woman to be awarded the Nobel Prize in Literature, in 1938. Born in the United States but raised in Zhenjiang, eastern China, Buck was an avid student of Chinese history and society, which contributed immensely to the vivid and detailed descriptions of Chinese life in her many novels. In addition to writing prolifically, Buck established Welcome House, the first international interracial adoption agency.

BOOK 45

FICTIONS
BY JORGE LUIS BORGES
December 22, 2008

To Stephen Harper,
Prime Minister of Canada,
A book you may or may not like,
From a Canadian writer,
With best wishes,
Yann Martel

Dear Mr. Harper,

I first read the short story collection *Fictions,* by the Argentinian writer Jorge Luis Borges (1899–1986), twenty years ago and I remember not liking it much. But Borges is a very famous writer from a continent with a rich literary tradition. No doubt my lack of appreciation indicated a lack in me, due to immaturity. Twenty years on, I would surely recognize its genius and I would join the legions of readers who hold Borges to be one of the great pens of the twentieth century.

Well, that change of opinion didn't take place. Upon rereading *Fictions* I was as unimpressed this time around as I remember being two decades ago.

These stories are intellectual games, literary forms of chess. They start simply enough, one pawn moving forward, so to speak, from fanciful premises—often about alternate worlds or fictitious books—that are then rigorously and organically developed by Borges till they reach a pitch of complexity that would please Bobby Fischer. Actually, the comparison to chess is not entirely right. Chess pieces, while moving around with great freedom, have fixed roles, established by a custom that is centuries old. Pawns move just so, as do rooks and knights and queens. With Borges, the chess pieces are played any which way, the rooks moving diagonally, the pawns laterally and so on. The result is stories that are surprising and inventive, but whose ideas can't be taken seriously because they aren't taken seriously by the author himself, who plays around with them *as if ideas didn't really matter.* And so the flashy but fraudulent erudition of *Fictions.* Let me give you one small example, taken at random. On page 68 of the story "The Library of Babel," which is about a universe shaped like an immense, infinite library, appears the following line concerning a particular book in that library:

> He showed his find to a traveling decipherer, who told him that the lines were written in Portuguese; others said it was Yiddish. Within the century experts had determined what the language actually was: a Samoyed-Lithuanian dialect of Guarani, with inflections from classical Arabic.

A Samoyed-Lithuanian dialect of Guarani, with inflections from classical Arabic? That's intellectually droll, in a nerdy way. There's a pleasure of the mind in seeing those languages unexpectedly juxtaposed. One mentally jumps around the map of the world. It's also, of course, linguistic nonsense. Samoyed and Lithuanian are from different language families—the first Uralic, the second Baltic—and so are unlikely ever to merge into a dialect, and even less so of Guarani, which is an indigenous language of South America. As for the inflections from classical Arabic, they involve yet another impossible leap over cultural and historical barriers. Do you see how this approach, if pursued relentlessly, makes a mockery of ideas? If ideas are mixed around like this for show and amusement, then they are ultimately reduced to show and amusement. And pursue this approach Borges does, line after line, page after page. His book is full of scholarly mumbo-jumbo that is ironic, magical, nonsensical. One of the games involved in *Fictions* is: do you get the references? If you do, you feel intelligent; if you don't, no worries, it's probably an invention, because much of the erudition in the book is invented. The only story that I found genuinely intellectually engaging, that is, making a serious, thought-provoking point, was "Three Versions of Judas," in which the character and theological implications of Judas are discussed. That story made me pause and think. Beyond the flash, there I found depth.

Borges is often described as a writer's writer. What this is supposed to mean is that writers will find in him all the finest qualities of the craft. I'm not sure I agree. By my reckoning, a great book increases one's involvement with the world. One seemingly turns away from the world when one reads a book, but only to see the world all the better once one has finished the book. Books, then, increase one's visual acuity of the world. With Borges, the more I read, the more the world was increasingly small and distant.

There's one characteristic that I noticed this time around that I hadn't the first time, and that is the extraordinary number of male names dropped into the narratives, most of them writers. The fictional world of Borges is nearly exclusively male unisexual. Women barely exist. The only female writers mentioned in *Fictions* are Dorothy Sayers, Agatha Christie and Gertrude Stein, the last two mentioned in "A Survey of the Works of Herbert Quain" to make a negative point. In "Pierre

Menard, Author of the *Quixote*," there is a Baroness de Bacourt and a Mme Henri Bachelier (note how Mme Bachelier's name is entirely concealed by her husband's). There may be a few others that I missed. Otherwise, the reader gets male friends and male writers and male characters into the multiple dozens. This is not merely a statistical feminist point. It hints rather at Borges's relationship to the world. The absence of women in his stories is matched by the absence of any intimate relations in them. Only in the last story, "The South," is there some warmth, some genuine pain to be felt between the characters. There is a failure in Borges to engage with the complexities of life, the complexities of conjugal or parental life, or, indeed, of any other emotional engagement. We have here a solitary male living entirely in his head, someone who refused to join the fray but instead hid in his books and spun one fantasy after another. And so my same, puzzled conclusion this time round after reading Borges: this is juvenile stuff.

Now why am I sending you a book that I don't like? For a good reason: because one should read widely, including books that one does not like. By so doing one avoids the possible pitfall of autodidacts, who risk shaping their reading to suit their limitations, thereby increasing those limitations. The advantage of structured learning, at the various schools available at all ages of one's life, is that one must measure one's intellect against systems of ideas that have been developed over centuries. One's mind is thus confronted with unsuspected new ideas.

Which is to say that one learns, one is shaped, as much by the books that one has liked as by those that one has disliked.

And there is also, of course, the possibility that you may love Borges. You may find his stories rich, deep, original and entertaining. You may think that I should try him again in another twenty years. Maybe then I'll be ready for Borges.

In the meantime, I wish you and your family a merry Christmas.

Yours truly,
Yann Martel

JORGE LUIS BORGES (1899–1986) was an Argentinian poet, short story writer, anthologist, critic, essayist and librarian. In his writings, he often explored the ideas of reality, philosophy, identity and time, frequently using the images of labyrinths and mirrors. Borges shared the 1961 Prix Formentor with Samuel Beckett, gaining international fame. In addition to writing and giving speaking engagements in the United States, Borges was the director of the National Library in Argentina, ironically gaining this position as he was losing his eyesight.

BOOK 46

BLACKBIRD SINGING:
POEMS AND LYRICS 1965–1999
BY PAUL McCARTNEY

January 5, 2009

To Stephen Harper,
Prime Minister of Canada,
Hey Jude,
From a Canadian writer,
With best wishes,
Yann Martel

Dear Mr. Harper,

Christmas crept up on me unnoticed this winter. Suddenly it was December 25 and I realized that I had committed that common, life-eating error: I had stopped paying heed to the flow of time. This lapse was reflected in the last book I sent you. Though original and imaginative, Borges's *Fictions* does not obviously fit with the original and imaginative books I sent you last Christmas (this is our *second* Christmas together, speaking of the flow of time). Those, if you remember, were three children's books: *The Brothers Lionheart, Imagine a Day,* and *The Mysteries of Harris Burdick*. They were suitably festive. Did you and your family enjoy them? Did they make you smile and laugh? This week I am sending you a book that I hope will genuinely please you, that you will unwrap, so to speak, and react to with surprise and delight. A real Christmas book, in other words.

I gather you are a Beatles fan. Here then is a selection of poems and lyrics by Paul McCartney. The songs he penned as a Beatle jumped out at me. I found it impossible to read "The Fool on the Hill" or "Eleanor Rigby" or "Lady Madonna" or "Maxwell's Silver Hammer" or "Lovely Rita" or "Rocky Raccoon" or "When I'm Sixty-Four," among others, in the hushed, even voice of normal prose. Instead, I sang along in my head, pausing at the right moments for the band to play its part. I'm not very familiar with McCartney's later career with Wings or as a solo artist, so those songs lay more quietly on the page for me, as did the poems. I could generally tell the lyrics from the poems because the former had more repetitions and something seemed lacking in them to give them independent literary life. It was in looking in the index that I would see that they were, most often, the words from a Wings song.

A song's lyrics, I realized, are inseparable from its melody. The melody supplies the *lift*, suspending one's disbelief and cynicism or giving one permission to entertain the forbidden, while the lyrics supply the *in*, inviting one to compare one's experience of life with what is being said in the song, or, even better, inviting one to sing along. The possibility of listening intelligibly and of singing along are essential to a song's appeal, because both involve the direct, personal participation of the listener. This participation, the extent to which one can mesh one's life and dreams with a song, explains why something so short— most of the Beatles' early songs are less than two minutes long—can go so deep so quickly. That's the beguiling illusion of a great song: it speaks to each of us individually, and with a magnetic voice, and so we listen intently, instantly drawn into an inner dream world. Who hasn't been moved to the core by a song, eyes closed and body shuddering with emotion? In that state, we address feelings we might be too shy to deal with in plain speech—raw, hungering lust, for example—or ones that cut deep but are so mundane we are embarrassed to talk about them: loneliness, yearning, heartbreak.

A good song is a hard trick to pull off. Classical musicians scoff at the crudeness of pop melodies, while more literary poets roll their eyes at the banality of pop lyrics, but there is a measure of envy in this resentment. What violinist or poet would not want a stadium full of rapt listeners? At any rate, Paul McCartney, with appealing lyrics and mesmerizing melodies, within the amazing creative synergy that was the Beatles, magisterially assisted by producer George Martin, pulled off that trick so well that every generation since the mid-sixties has fallen in love with his songs. But you already know that.

Yours truly,
Yann Martel

PAUL MCCARTNEY (b. 1942) has been a musical icon for nearly fifty years, penning songs, movie soundtracks and orchestral arrangements. He remains most famous as a member of the Beatles, for whom, with John Lennon, he wrote some of his best songs. His success continued after the breakup of the band in 1970. Performing with Wings, and as a solo artist, McCartney has maintained his status as one of the most prolific and talented musicians of all time. He is also known for his animal rights activism.

BOOK 47

THE LESSER EVIL:
POLITICAL ETHICS IN AN AGE OF TERROR
BY MICHAEL IGNATIEFF

January 19, 2009

To Stephen Harper,
Prime Minister of Canada,
A book for a leader by a leader,
From a Canadian writer,
With best wishes,
Yann Martel

Dear Mr. Harper,

Okay, back to work, for you and for me. I'm rewriting my next book, for the third and last time I hope, and a new session of Parliament is opening soon. We both face a busy winter.

I believe you said in an interview not long ago that you hadn't read much of Michael Ignatieff's work. It's obvious that you should, isn't it? After all, you will be facing him every day in the House of Commons this year—he may even take your job—so it would be to your advantage to get to know his mind. The man has an impressive c.v., I must say. Degrees from the University of Toronto, Oxford, Harvard; teaching positions at Cambridge, Hautes Études in Paris, Harvard; a career in broadcasting and journalism; sixteen books to his credit (including three novels)—I can't think of an aspiring Canadian prime minister with a resumé to match. There have been prime ministers who were well educated and prime ministers who have written books, but none to this extent. Does that mean he would make a peerless prime minister? Of course not. Leadership can't be reduced to academic credentials or books on a shelf. Personality, vision, instinct, people skills, practical knowledge, toughness, resilience, rhetorical flair, charisma, luck—there is much that goes into the making of a political leader besides grey matter.

Having said that, a formidable intellect can only help, especially if it has been tested in practical ways, as Mr. Ignatieff's has. There's been little of the proverbial ivory tower in the years before he was elected to Parliament. His concern for human rights and democracy are real, not theoretical. He has travelled to many troubled spots on this planet to try to answer that essential question: how best can a society govern itself? Should Mr. Ignatieff ever move into 24 Sussex Drive, the gain for Canadians will no doubt be public policy goals that are sound and enlightened. Will he be able to bring these goals about? Will he know when to listen, when to compromise, when to act decisively? Many a politician has come to power with set ideas on how to fix things, only to find reality either more complex or more resistant than they had anticipated. We'll find out in the coming months how Michael Ignatieff fares.

In the meantime, to help you not only in dealing with the new Leader of Her Majesty's Loyal Opposition but also as an aid in setting policy, I am sending you *The Lesser Evil: Political Ethics in an Age of Terror*, a more recent book by your fellow parliamentarian, published in 2004. The cover seems uninspiring. It was chosen for a good reason: it's a photograph of a staircase at Auschwitz. Up and down those stairs went people who were in the grip of political ethics gone terribly wrong. As I said, there's nothing abstract about Mr. Ignatieff's concerns. He looks at real-life political dilemmas and seeks to find out what went wrong and how those wrongs might be made right.

The Lesser Evil is a study on liberal democracies and terrorism. How do people who value freedom and dignity handle those who commit senseless violence against them? What is the right balance between the competing demands of rights and security? What can a democratic society allow itself to do and still call itself democratic? These are some of the questions that Mr. Ignatieff tries to answer. He looks at nations as diverse as Russia, the United Kingdom, the U.S., Germany, Italy, Spain, Sri Lanka, Chile, Argentina, Israel and Palestine, in their current state but also historically, to see how they have dealt with assaults by terrorists. He also makes literary references, to Dostoyevsky and Conrad, to Euripides and Homer. Throughout, the approach is open, fair and critical, the analysis is rigorous and insightful, the conclusions are wise. Last but not least, the style is engaging. Mr. Ignatieff has a fine pen. My favourite line in the book is this one, on page 121: "Liberal states cannot be protected by herbivores."

Mr. Ignatieff is a passionate yet subtle defender of liberal democracies and he finds that generally the tools they already have at their disposal will do in times of terrorist threat. Indeed, he argues that overreaction to a threat can do more long-term harm to a liberal democracy than the threat itself. The U.S. Patriot Act and Canada's Bill C-36 are two examples Mr. Ignatieff gives of well-meaning but redundant and misguided attempts to deal with terrorism. When the regular tools won't do, he acknowledges that the choices faced by liberal democracies are difficult. He makes the case that when a society that values freedom and human dignity is confronted with a threat to its existence, it must move beyond rigid moral perfectionism or outright utilitarian necessity and—carefully, mindfully, vigilantly—follow a path of lesser evil, that is, allow itself to commit some infringements of the part in order to save the whole. It is a position that seeks to reconcile the *realism* necessary to fight terrorism with the *idealism* of our democratic values. To work one's way through such treacherous ground, to get down to details and talk about torture and preemptive military action, to give just two examples, requires a mind that is tough, sharp and brave. I'm glad to say that Mr. Ignatieff has such a mind.

Yours truly,
Yann Martel

MICHAEL IGNATIEFF (b. 1947) is the leader of the Liberal Party of Canada. Prior to his political career, Ignatieff held several prominent positions in academia and broadcasting. He has been on the faculty of the universities of Oxford, Cambridge and Toronto, and was the director from 2000 to 2005 of Harvard's Carr Centre for Human Rights Policy. During his time in England, he worked as a documentary filmmaker and political commentator with the BBC. Ignatieff is the author of sixteen books, including a biography of Isaiah Berlin and three novels.

BOOK 48

GILEAD
BY MARILYNNE ROBINSON
February 2, 2009

To Stephen Harper,
Prime Minister of Canada,
An Obama pick,
From a Canadian writer,
With best wishes,
Yann Martel

Dear Mr. Harper,

Well, with a budget like that, you might as well be a socialist. Remarkable how much your government has vowed to spend. Your days as a radical Reformer, determined to shrink the government like a wool sweater in a hot water wash, must be from a former life. I wonder what your friends at the National Citizens Coalition think? (Why is there no apostrophe in the name of that organization? I checked their website and that's how they spell it. Are they so committed to free enterprise and fearful of social commitment that they won't put the Citizens in the possessive case?)

I gather Michael Ignatieff was amused to hear echoes of his own statements in the recent Speech from the Throne (I enclose a *Globe and Mail* article). Don't worry, you're not the only one echoing him. President Obama (I do like the ring of that), in explaining why he was closing down the detention camp at Guantanamo Bay and the CIA's secret overseas prisons and repealing other dubious counterterrorism measures taken by George W. Bush, used words that could have been Mr. Ignatieff's. How our liberal democratic ideals must be reflected in our actions, how we cannot lightly sacrifice rights for the sake of excessive security expediency, how we will triumph over our enemies by keeping faith with our ideals, not by abandoning them, and so on—it's all entirely in the spirit of the forty-seventh book in our library, *The Lesser Evil*. Clearly Mr. Ignatieff's views are shared by many, influenced by and feeding into a current of thought that is now becoming widely accepted, so you do well to open yourself to it.

Speaking of President Obama, it's because of him that I'm sending you the novel *Gilead*, by the American writer Marilynne Robinson. It's one of his favourite novels. It turns out Barack Obama is a reader, a big reader. And the books he has read and cherished have not only been practical texts that someone interested in governance would likely favour. No, he also likes poetry, fiction, philosophy: the Bible, Shakespeare's tragedies, Melville, Toni Morrison, Doris Lessing, the poets Elizabeth Alexander and Derek Walcott, the philosophers Reinhold Niebuhr and St. Augustine, and many more. They've formed his oratory, his thinking, his very being. He's a man-built-by-words and he has impressed the whole world.

I would sincerely recommend that you read *Gilead* before you meet President Obama on February 19. For two people who are meeting for the first time, there's nothing like talking about a book that both have read to create common ground and a sense of intimacy, of knowing the other in a small but important way. After all, to like the same book implies a similar emotional response to it, a shared recognition of the world reflected in it. This is assuming, of course, that you like the book.

That shouldn't be too hard. There is much to like in *Gilead*. It's a slow, honest novel, suffused with wonder and amazement (those two words come up often in the book), and surprisingly religious, practically devotional. There are no chapters, just entries divided by a blank line, as if it were a diary. The narration is leisurely and episodic, giving the impression of a ramble, but it's actually a carefully constructed novel, building in power as it goes along. There is no facile irony, no seeking to please by the easy recourse of humour. Instead, the tone is sober, gentle, intelligent. The story is told by John Ames, an aged preacher who is ill with a heart condition that will kill him soon enough. He has a seven-year-old son come to him late in life as a result of an autumnal marriage to a much younger, much loved woman. He wants his son to know something of his father, and of his father's father, and of his father's father's father—all of them named John Ames and all of them preachers—so he writes a long letter for his son to read when he is of age. The style is on the surface effortless, a plain, poetic speech with much about God and God's people and the meaning of it all, with a few references to baseball. Very American, then, a novel one could imagine Ralph Waldo Emerson having written if Emerson had written fiction. *Gilead* is a graceful work, suffused with grace, and it has the luminous feel of the profound. It's a book that aspires to be a church, quiet, sparely furnished, whitely lit, filled with Presence and steeped in the essential. If there's a novel that should give you a sense of stillness, it is this one.

I hope you like it. And if you don't, remember nonetheless that it is one of the keys that will let you into the mind of the current President of the United States.

Yours truly,
Yann Martel

MARILYNNE ROBINSON (b. 1943) is the American author of two works of non-fiction, *Mother Country* and *The Death of Adam*, and three novels. Her first novel, *Housekeeping*, won a Hemingway Foundation/PEN Award and earned her a nomination for the Pulitzer Prize for Fiction. Her second novel, *Gilead*, won several awards including the Pulitzer Prize for Fiction, the National Book Critics Circle Award for Fiction and the Ambassador Book Award. Robinson earned a Ph.D. from the University of Washington and at present teaches at the Iowa Writers' Workshop.

BOOK 49

THE OLD MAN AND THE SEA
BY ERNEST HEMINGWAY

February 16, 2009

To Stephen Harper,
Prime Minister of Canada,
From a Canadian writer,
With best wishes,
Yann Martel

Dear Mr. Harper,

The famous Ernest Hemingway. *The Old Man and the Sea* is one of those works of literature that most everyone has heard of, even those who haven't read it. Despite its brevity—127 pages in the well-spaced edition I am sending you—it's had a lasting effect on English literature, as has Hemingway's work in general. I'd say that his short stories, gathered in the collections *In Our Time*, *Men without Women* and *Winner Take Nothing*, among others, are his greatest achievement—and above all, the story "Big Two-Hearted River"—but his novels *The Sun Also Rises*, *A Farewell to Arms* and *For Whom the Bell Tolls* are more widely read.

The greatness of Hemingway lies not so much in what he said as how he said it. He took the English language and wrote it in a way that no one had written it before. If you compare Hemingway, who was born in 1899, and Henry James, who died in 1916, that overlap of seventeen years seems astonishing, so contrasting are their styles. With James, truth, verisimilitude, realism, whatever you want to call it, is achieved by a baroque abundance of language. Hemingway's style is the exact opposite. He stripped the language of ornamentation, prescribing adjectives and adverbs to his prose the way a careful doctor would prescribe pills to a hypochondriac. The result was prose of revolutionary terseness, with a cadence, vigour and elemental simplicity that bring to mind a much older text: the Bible.

That combination is not fortuitous. Hemingway was well versed in biblical language and imagery and *The Old Man and the Sea* can be read as a Christian allegory, though I wouldn't call it a religious work, certainly not in the way the book I sent you two weeks ago, *Gilead,* is. Rather, Hemingway uses Christ's passage on Earth in a secular way to explore the meaning of human suffering. "Grace under pressure" was the formulation Hemingway offered when he was asked what he meant by "guts" in describing the grit shown by many of his characters. Another way of putting that would be the achieving of victory through defeat, which matches more deeply, I think, the Christ-like odyssey of Santiago, the old man of the title. For concerning Christ, that was the Apostle Paul's momentous insight (some would call it God's gift): the possibility of triumph, of salvation, in the very midst of ruination. It's a message, a belief, that transforms the human experience entirely. Career failures, family disasters, accidents, disease, old age—these human experiences that might otherwise be tragically final instead become threshold events.

As I was thinking about Santiago and his epic encounter with the great marlin, I wondered whether there was any political dimension to his story. I came to the conclusion that there isn't. In politics, victory comes through victory and defeat only brings defeat. The message of Hemingway's poor Cuban fisherman is purely personal, addressing the individual in each one of us and not the roles we might take on. Despite its vast exterior setting, *The Old Man and the Sea* is an intimate work of the soul. And so I wish upon you what I wish upon all of us: that our return from the high seas be as dignified as Santiago's.

Yours truly,
Yann Martel

ERNEST HEMINGWAY (1899–1961) was an American journalist, novelist and short story writer. He is internationally acclaimed for his works *The Sun Also Rises, A Farewell to Arms, For Whom the Bell Tolls* and his Pulitzer Prize–winning novella, *The Old Man and the Sea*. Hemingway's writing style is characteristically straightforward and understated, featuring tightly constructed prose. He drove an ambulance in World War I, and was a key figure in the circle of expatriate artists and writers in Paris in the 1920s known as the "Lost Generation." Hemingway won the Nobel Prize in Literature in 1954.

BOOK 50

JANE AUSTEN: A LIFE
BY CAROL SHIELDS

March 2, 2009

To Stephen Harper,
Prime Minister of Canada,
Our fiftieth book,
From a Canadian writer,
With best wishes,
Yann Martel

Dear Mr. Harper,

The gentle yet probing questioning, the lightness of touch, the accuracy of statement, the keen moral awareness, the constant intelligence—finally, it's only Jane Austen's irony that is missing from this excellent look at her life by Carol Shields, which is fitting since a fair-minded biography isn't the most suitable place for broad irony. Otherwise, without any attempt at imitation or pastiche, this book is so much in the spirit of its subject, so intimately concerned with the meaning of being a writer, that one can nearly imagine that one is reading *Carol Shields: A Life*, by Jane Austen. Not that Carol Shields intrudes on the text in an unseemly way. Not at all. Aside from the brief prologue, the personal pronoun *I* to designate the biographer never appears. This book is entirely a biography of Jane Austen. But the spirit of the two, of the English novelist who lived between 1775 and 1817 and of the Canadian novelist who lived between 1935 and 2003, are so kindred that the book exudes a feeling of friendship rather than of analysis.

The illusion of complicity is helped by the fact that not very much is known about Jane Austen, despite her being the author of six novels that sit with full rights in the library of great English literature. She wrote *Pride and Prejudice, Sense and Sensibility, Northanger Abbey, Mansfield Park, Emma* and *Persuasion* in unremitting rural obscurity. She became a published writer only six years before her death and the four novels that came out during her lifetime were published anonymously, the author being described only as "a Lady." And even when it became widely known after her death that the lady in question had been one Jane Austen, resident of the village of Chawton, in Hampshire, posterity didn't find out much more about her. Jane Austen never met another published writer, was never interviewed by a journalist and never moved in a literary circle beyond the completely personal one of her family, who were her first and most loyal readers. What we might have found out about her through her letters is partial, since many were destroyed by her sister Cassandra. In other words, Jane Austen lived among people who hardly took note of her, and I mean that literally: except for some few family members and friends, very little was written about Jane Austen during her lifetime that might have allowed us to become acquainted with her. A biography of such an elusive person will therefore have more the character of a spiritual quest than of a factual account. Therein lies the excellence of Shields's biography. It is not cluttered by facts. It is rather a meditation on the writerly existence of Jane Austen—and who better to do that than a writer who can be viewed as a modern incarnation of her? Carol Shields had a similar interest in the female perspective and was as comfortable as Jane Austen in exploring the domestic and the intimate, plumbing its depths until the universal was revealed. The intuitive rightness of her biography amply makes up for the dearth of hard facts.

The eleventh book I sent you was a Jane Austen novel, though a minor one because unfinished, *The Watsons*, if you remember. If that's the only Austen you've read, you don't have to worry that you will be left in the dark by this biography. It's called *Jane Austen: A Life*, after all, and not *Jane Austen: Her Books*. Of course, her books are discussed, but only to the extent that they shed light on their author. The reader doesn't have to have an intimate knowledge of them to appreciate what Shields is discussing.

This book is a real pleasure to read, I must emphasize that. It is intelligent in a most engaging way, not only making Jane

n front of the Jane Austen Centre.

Austen better known to us, but also bringing the reader in on the alchemical process of writing. Jane Austen, unlimited by her tightly circumscribed life, composed novels that still speak to readers today, whose lives, especially that of her female readers, have changed vastly. Carol Shields, for her part, unlimited by the poverty of source material, composed a biography that speaks to everyone, male or female, devoted Austen reader or neophyte. I hope you will enjoy it, this, the fiftieth book that we have shared.

I was in Bath recently, where Jane Austen lived for a few years. She was miserable while there, but it's a lovely town nonetheless. I took a picture for you, which I include with this letter.

Yours truly,
Yann Martel

CAROL SHIELDS (1935–2003) was an American-Canadian poet, novelist, professor and critic. Her works include ten novels and two collections of short stories. During her literary career, Shields was a professor at the University of Ottawa, the University of British Columbia, the University of Manitoba and the University of Winnipeg, where she also served as chancellor. She is best remembered for her highly acclaimed novel *The Stone Diaries*, which won the Pulitzer Prize and the Governor General's Literary Award. Her biography of Jane Austen won the Charles Taylor Prize for Non-Fiction.

BOOK 51

JULIUS CAESAR
BY WILLIAM SHAKESPEARE
March 16, 2009

To Stephen Harper,
Prime Minister of Canada,
S.O.S. (Save Our Shakespeare),
From a Canadian writer,
With best wishes,
Yann Martel

Dear Mr. Harper,

Yesterday was the Ides of March, and so *Julius Caesar,* by William Shakespeare. There is nothing sacred in or about Shakespeare, but one can lose and find oneself in his work the way one can lose and find oneself in the Bible. Both are full worlds, one secular, the other religious, and both have spawned generations of readers and scholars who can quote chapter and verse from any given book or play. If one were on a desert island with only the Bible or the complete works of Shakespeare, one would do all right. If one had both, one would do well.

There is everything in Shakespeare (including dullness in the history plays). The English language and the nature of drama were still on the anvil in the smithy when Shakespeare was around, which was between the years 1564 and 1616, and the formative beatings of his hammer mark to this day the English language, theatre, and our view of the world. To give you just two small examples: in Act I, towards the end of Scene II,

Cassius asks Casca if Cicero had anything to say about Caesar fainting. Cicero did, but in Greek. Casca deadpans, "It was Greek to me." Later, in Act III, Scene I, Caesar is making clear that his will is firm and that he is not easily put off his course. He is, he says, "constant as the northern star." These are but two of the many expressions that Shakespeare brought to the language he was working in. He brought more than that, of course. His plays, besides being vivid and dramatic, overflow with insights into the human condition. The adjective "Shakespearean" is a broad one. If that single man was a spring, we now all live in his delta.

Julius Caesar is a play about politics, more specifically about power. The potential power of one individual, the power of tradition, the power of principles, the power of persuasion, the power of the masses—all these powers clash in the play, to deadly effect. Shakespeare takes no sides. His play is a tragedy, but it is not only Caesar's tragedy. It is also the tragedy of Brutus and Cassius, of Portia and Calpurnia, of Cinna the Poet, of Rome itself.

Since *Julius Caesar* is about power and politics, we might as well talk about power and politics. Let me discuss concerns I have with two decisions your government recently announced.

My first concern is about the Social Sciences and Humanities Research Council. New money allocated to the Council is apparently to be spent exclusively on "business-related degrees." Don't you feel that there's a measure of contradiction between the libertarian, small-government ideals of your party and telling an arm's-length body how to spend its money? Aren't you making government bigger and more intrusive by doing so? But that's an aside. More troubling is the denaturing of SSHRC's role. I've never understood why public universities, funded by the taxpayer, should necessarily have business departments. Is making money really an academic discipline?

Don't get me wrong; there's nothing shameful about money, or the making of it, but we're losing sight of the purpose of a university if we think it's the place to churn out MBAs. A university is the repository and crucible of a society, the place where it studies itself. It is the brain of a society. It is not the wallet. Businesses come and go. Shakespeare doesn't. A university builds minds and souls. A business employs. The world would be a better place if rather than having business types infiltrating universities, we had Shakespeare types infiltrating businesses. I imagine this line of argument is falling on your deaf ear. Perhaps I've misunderstood. To paraphrase Antony speaking of Brutus, you are an honourable man and you must know what you're doing.

My second concern is the announcement by the Canadian Heritage Minister James Moore that funding from the new Canadian Periodical Fund might be restricted to those magazines that have a circulation greater than five thousand. That will pretty well kill off every single arts and literary magazine in Canada. "Good thing," you might be thinking. "Elitist little rags, who needs them?" Well, we all need them, because good things start small. I'll give you just one example: my own. I was first published by the *Malahat Review*, which comes out of Victoria, B.C. Their early support, when I was in my twenties, galvanized me. It made me want to write more and to write better. It's because I was published in the *Malahat* that I won my first literary award, that I met my literary agent, that I came to the attention of Toronto publishers. The *Malahat* is where I was born as a writer. If it goes, so does the next generation of writers and poets. But perhaps I've misunderstood. You are an honourable man and you must know what you're doing.

Turning SSHRC into an MBA funding agency and eliminating arts and literary magazines are incomprehensible measures to me. The sums involved are so small relatively, yet the purposes they serve so important. Is it really your aim to transform Canada into a post-literate society? As it is, many young people are post-historical and post-religious. If literacy is the next pillar to go, what will be left of our identity? But perhaps I've misunderstood. You are an honourable man and you must know what you're doing.

In Act III, Scene 3 of *Caesar,* you will meet Cinna the Poet. He is torn to pieces by the rabble, who mistake him for another Cinna, one of the conspirators. That is not the Canadian way. Here in Canada, at this time, it is the Canadian government that is attacking Cinna the Poet. But perhaps I've misunderstood. You are an honourable man and you must know what you're doing.

Yours truly,
Yann Martel

WILLIAM SHAKESPEARE (1564–1616) wrote plays and poems.

BOOK 52

BURNING ICE: ART & CLIMATE CHANGE
A COLLABORATION ORGANIZED
BY DAVID BUCKLAND
AND THE CAPE FAREWELL FOUNDATION

March 30, 2009

To Stephen Harper,
Prime Minister of Canada,
A book on a hot topic,
From a Canadian writer,
With best wishes,
Yann Martel

Dear Mr. Harper,

I had never heard of Cape Farewell, a British NGO, until an e-mail from them popped into my inbox. They were inviting me, thanks to funding by the Musagetes Foundation here in Canada, on a trip they were organizing to Peru. To explain their organization and its objectives, they offered to send me a book and a DVD. I was intrigued and so accepted. What did I have to lose? A few days later, said book and DVD arrived in the mail. I read the book, watched the DVD, checked out their website (www.capefarewell.com) and promptly wrote to Cape Farewell to accept their invitation.

Many people were first introduced to climate change by *An Inconvenient Truth*, the movie based on the touring presentation by Al Gore. Cape Farewell's mission is to move beyond that initial awareness and orchestrate a cultural response to climate change. To do that, they organize expeditions to the frontiers of climate change, those hot spots (literally) where the change is most apparent. Scientists are there too, doing their research, and so artists can see both climate change's theatre and some of its actors. The artists are then invited to respond, to become actors themselves. The DVD *Art from a Changing Arctic* documents the first three Cape Farewell expeditions to Svalbard, while *Burning Ice* records some of the responses by the artists.

It's a varied book, as you'll see. There is visual art, both photographic, pictorial and sculptural, there are essays, both scientific, giving a good recap about climate change, and personal, relating the reactions of individuals to that change. *Burning Ice* came out in 2006 and it's already out of date. In one essay, a scientist states that by 2050 there will be no more summer ice in the Arctic. Scientists are now predicting such a disappearance by 2013. Only three years on and matters have already gotten worse. It's easy to fall into pessimism when contemplating climate change. "Such a global calamity—what can I do?" The great quality of *Burning Ice* is that it shows what can be done: one can respond. Of course, a painting, a photograph, a string of words won't save the planet. But it's the beginning of coming to grips with the issue. Climate change on its own is an impersonal force, deeply disempowering. Art inspired by climate change, because the making of art is personally involving, a whole-person activity, is empowering, both for the maker and the spectator.

As I flipped through the pages of *Burning Ice*, gazing at the artwork, reading the essays, I marvelled and I was distressed: an odd mixture, but a step up from simply feeling distress. Whether the art that Cape Farewell generates, to be seen in books and exhibitions, turns out to be elegiac, a farewell to our planet, or the beginning of real change in the way we live, will only be seen in years to come. But one thing is certain: our response to climate change cannot be purely political. Politicians have been dragging their feet—you among them—because of the power of the carbon-fuel industrial complex. It is citizens who must move first, and art is an ideal way to help them do that. Art wrestles with its subject matter on a level that the individual, the man, woman, teenager and child on the street, can engage with and react to. Once citizens are involved in the vital issue of climate change, politicians will have to follow their lead.

You might as well get ahead of the wave. I hope you are both moved and alarmed by *Burning Ice*.

Yours truly,
Yann Martel

DAVID BUCKLAND is a British artist specializing in photography, portraiture, and set and costume design for theatrical productions. Many of his works have been exhibited in major galleries around the world, including the Centre Georges Pompidou in Paris and the Metropolitan Museum of Art in New York. Buckland is also the founder of the Cape Farewell Project, a community of artists, scientists and communicators committed to raising cultural awareness through artistic response to climate change.

LOUIS RIEL
BY CHESTER BROWN
AND
**THE SAILOR WHO FELL FROM GRACE
WITH THE SEA**
BY YUKIO MISHIMA
translated by John Nathan
April 13, 2009

for *Louis Riel*
To Stephen Harper,
Prime Minister of Canada,
A graphic novel on a key episode
in Canadian history,
From a Canadian writer,
With best wishes,
Yann Martel

for *The Sailor Who Fell from
Grace with the Sea*
To Stephen Harper,
Prime Minister of Canada,
A graphic novel of a different kind,
From a Canadian writer,
With best wishes,
Yann Martel

Dear Mr. Harper,

When I started sending you books, I said they would be books that would "inspire stillness." A book is a marvellous tool—in fact, a unique tool—to increase one's depth of reflection, to help one think and feel. It takes a long time and great effort to write a good book, whether of fiction or non-fiction. It's not only the preliminary research; there are also the weeks and months of thinking. When asked how long it took them to write a book, I've heard writers say, "My whole life." I know what they mean by that. Their entire being went into the writing of that book, and the few years it actually took to get it down on the page were only the tip of the proverbial iceberg. It's not surprising that such a lengthy process, akin to the maturing of a good wine, should yield a rich product worthy of careful consideration.

But the stillness that books can induce does not mean they are peaceable. Stillness is not the same thing as tranquility. You might have noticed that a few weeks ago with *Julius Caesar*. There's hardly any peace and tranquility in that play, yet it is thought-provoking nonetheless, isn't it?

That stillness out of turmoil continues with the two books I am sending you this week. I'm sure you are familiar with the tragic saga of Louis Riel. The English hated him, the French loved him. Of course, I don't mean the English and French of Europe when I say that. I mean the people from that nation that materialized north of the United States. The English and Irish and Scottish of Ontario were newly calling themselves Canadians, while the French-speaking Métis of the Red River Settlement were not. In one man, the tensions and resentments of a new nation were symbolized. It was a complicated mess whose effects are felt to this day. Would the Parti Québécois have been elected in 1976 had Louis Riel and the Red River Métis been treated more fairly by Ottawa? Or would that have led Ontarians to elect an "Ontario Party" advocating union with the United States? What is clear—and you must surely know this from your own personal experience in politics—is that once prejudice and bad faith are entrenched among a people, it's very hard to get them to get along.

Louis Riel, by the Canadian graphic artist Chester Brown, is a serious work that tells a serious story in a thoughtful and evocative manner. The drawings are compelling and the storytelling is both gripping and subtle. Louis Riel comes across as he likely was: a strange and charismatic man, religiously crazy at times but also genuinely concerned about the fate of his Métis people.

The description "strange and charismatic" could also be applied to the Japanese writer Yukio Mishima (1925–1970). If Riel was religiously crazy, then Mishima was aesthetically crazy. You might have heard about how Mishima died. He's as well known for his death as he is for his writings. The life of an author should not normally be conflated with his work, but a healthy writer who, at the age of forty-five and at the height of his fame, commits suicide by ritual disembowelment and beheading— what is popularly called *harakiri*—after taking over a military base and exhorting the army of his country to overthrow the government, cannot but attract attention for reasons other than his books. In this case, life and work are intimately linked. Mishima's end had less to do with politics and restoring Japan to a supposed former glory than with personal notions he had about death and beauty. He was obsessed by death and beauty. The characters in his novel *The Sailor Who Fell from Grace with the Sea*—Fusako, the mother; Noboru, her son; and Ryuji, the sailor—demonstrate this. They are exquisitely realized. One gets a sense of them not only in their physical being but in their inner makeup too. All are, in their different ways, beautiful. And yet their story is riven by violence and death. I won't say anything more.

I'll confess that when I first read *The Sailor Who Fell from Grace with the Sea* in my early twenties, I hated it because I loved it. It and Knut Hamsun's *Hunger* are the only masterpieces I've read with the breathless feeling that I possibly could have written them myself. Those two stories were in me, I felt, but a Japanese writer and a Norwegian writer got to them before I could.

I should explain why I am sending you two books this week. I'm off on a holiday and don't want to worry about books being lost in the mail. So these are your April books, *Louis Riel* for April 13 and *The Sailor Who Fell from Grace with the Sea* for April 27.

How curious and unrelated they seem. I doubt Mishima had ever heard of Louis Riel, and there's nothing in *Louis Riel* to make me think that Chester Brown is an admirer of Mishima. But I've always liked that about books, how they can be so different from each other and yet rest together without strife on a bookshelf. The hope of literature, the hope of stillness, is that the peace with which the most varied books can lie side by side will transform their readers, so that they too will be able to live side by side with people very different from themselves.

Yours truly,
Yann Martel

Reply: April 29, 2009

Dear Mr. Martel,

On behalf of the Right Honourable Stephen Harper, I would like to acknowledge receipt of your correspondence, with which you enclosed a copy of *The Sailor Who Fell from Grace with the Sea* by Yukio Mishima and a copy of *Louis Riel, A Comic-Strip Biography* by Chester Brown.

The Prime Minister wishes me to convey his thanks for sending him these books. You may be assured that your thoughtful gesture is most appreciated.

Yours truly,
S. Russell
Executive Correspondence Officer

CHESTER BROWN (b. 1960) is a Canadian cartoonist who is part of the alternative comics movement and the creator of several graphic novels and comic series. His comics are generally grim, classified in the genres of horror, surrealism and black comedy and focusing on darker subjects like mental health issues and cannibalism. His best-known work, *Louis Riel: A Comic-Strip Biography,* was five years in the making. Some of his other works include *The Playboy, I Never Liked You* and the comic book series *Yummy Fur* and *Underwater.* Born and raised in Montreal, Brown now lives in Toronto.

YUKIO MISHIMA (1925–1970), born Kimitake Hiraoka, was a Japanese novelist, short story writer, poet and traditional kabuki playwright. His best-known novels, *Confessions of a Mask, The Temple of the Golden Pavilion, The Sailor Who Fell from Grace with the Sea* and the *Sea of Fertility* quartet, have insured his enduring fame in Japan and around the world. Mishima committed suicide after taking over a military base with his own private army, ostensibly as a protest over Japan's drift away from its traditional values.

BOOK 55

THE GIFT
BY LEWIS HYDE
May 11, 2009

To Stephen Harper,
Prime Minister of Canada,
A gift to be shared, like all gifts,
From a Canadian writer,
With best wishes,
Yann Martel

Dear Mr. Harper,

One of the strengths of non-fiction is its ability to focus. Whereas fiction can be as broad as the humanities, non-fiction tends to specialize, like a science. Writers of fiction commonly hear from their editors that they must "show, not tell." They must do so because fiction creates new, unfamiliar worlds that must be felt and not only described. Non-fiction, on the other hand, relies on a world already in existence, our own, with its true history and real historical figures. Of course, that history and those figures must be made to breathe with life on the page; good writing is always essential. Nonetheless, that basis in the factual world frees non-fiction writers from the cumbersome task of wholly inventing characters and situations and gives them far more liberty to straight-out tell. What is gained is an ability to cover a single topic deeply. What is lost is broad appeal. With non-fiction, the reader must be more actively interested in the subject covered. For example, a history of feudal Japan will likely attract fewer readers than a novel about feudal Japan. Such was the case, at least, with James Clavell's novel *Shogun* and I don't think it's unusual.

The result of this specialization is that the world of non-fiction is more fragmented. A novel is more like another novel than a work of non-fiction is like another work of non-fiction. Proof of that is in the names we give to these categories: we know what fiction is, so we call it that, and under the label we comfortably place the plays, poems, novels and short stories of the world. But what about those books that aren't fiction? Well, we're not so sure what they are, so we define them by what they are not: they are *non*-fiction. The result of this lack of convention, with great non-fiction, is a high degree of originality.

A sterling example of how original non-fiction can be is the book I am sending you this week. In *The Gift*, Lewis Hyde looks at the meaning and consequence of a gift, that is, of an object or service that is given for nothing, freely, without expectation of a concrete or immediate return. With that single notion in mind, Hyde evokes an array of peoples, places and practices and makes a coherent whole of what would be a novelistic mess. You'll see for yourself. The Puritans in America, Irish and Bengali folklore, the Trobriand Islanders off New Guinea, the Maori of New Zealand, the potlatch of the Pacific Coast First Nations, Alcoholics Anonymous, tales of Buddha, the Ford Motor Company, the fate of unexpected sums of money in an urban ghetto of Chicago, Martin Luther, John Calvin, the lives of Walt Whitman and Ezra Pound, to mention just a few references that I remember—all are woven together as Hyde lays out his thesis on the differences between the exchange of gifts and the exchange of commodities. The currencies involved in these trades are radically different. In the first, sentiments are exchanged; in the second, money. The first creates attachment; the second, detachment. The first creates a community; the second, liberty. The first builds capital that does not circulate; the second loses its value if it does not keep moving. These ideas are examined in the light of the many anthropological and sociological examples in the book.

Art is at the heart of *The Gift*. Hyde sees every aspect of art as a gift: creativity is received as a gift by the artist, art is made as a gift and then, rather awkwardly in our current economic system, art is traded as a gift. That certainly rings true with me. I have never thought of my creativity in monetary terms. I write now as I did when I started, for nothing. And yet the artist must live. How then to quantify the value of one's art? How do we correlate a poem's worth with a monetary value? I use the word again: it's awkward. If Hyde favours the spirit of gift-giving over that of commercial exchange, it's not because he's a doctrinaire idealist. He's not. But it's clear what he thinks: we've forgotten the spirit of the gift in our commodity-driven society and the cost of that has been the parching of our souls.

The Gift is a refreshment to the dried-up soul. For Lewis Hyde, the spirit of the gift goes far beyond Christmas and birthdays. It's actually a philosophy. And it's hard not to adhere to it after reading hundreds of pages on gift-making and gift-giving in all corners of the world. Perhaps we have forgotten a little how good it feels to give freely, how what is given to us must be passed on, so that the gift can live on, swimming about human communities like a fish, always alive so long as it keeps moving. Perhaps that's why the things we value the most are often those that we were given. Perhaps that is our more natural mode of exchange. At the very least, after reading this book you'll never think of the word "gift" in the same way.

One last point, made in the spirit of Hyde's book. I have now sent you fifty-seven books of all types, and there will be more to come, as long as you are Prime Minister. I imagine these books are lying on a shelf somewhere in your offices. But they won't be there forever. One day you will leave office and you'll take with you the extensive paper trail that a prime minister creates. That trail will be placed in hundreds of cardboard boxes that will end up at the National Archives of Canada, where in time they will be opened and the contents parsed by scholars. I would feel sad if that were the fate of the books I have given you. Novels and poems and plays are not meant to live in cardboard boxes. Like all gifts, they should be shared. So may I suggest that you share what I have shared with you. One by one, or all together, as you wish, give the books away, with only two conditions: first, that they not be kept permanently by each recipient but rather passed on in a timely fashion, after they've been read, and, second, that they never be sold. That would keep the gift-giving spirit of our book club alive.

Yours truly,
Yann Martel

P.S. Could you please thank S. Russell on my behalf for his or her reply for the last books I sent you, the Mishima and the Chester Brown. [See the REPLY *section of Books 53 and 54.]*

LEWIS HYDE (b. 1945) is an American poet, translator, essayist and cultural critic. He has edited a book of essays by Henry David Thoreau and translated the poems of the Nobel Prize–winning Spanish poet Vicente Aleixandre. He has also written a work of cultural criticism, *Trickster Makes This World*, and a collection of poems, *This Error Is the Sign of Love*. Formerly an instructor at Harvard University, Hyde now teaches writing at Kenyon College and is a Fellow at Harvard's Berkman Center for Internet and Society

LIST OF AUTHORS AND TITLES

YANN MARTEL was born in Spain in 1963. After studying philosophy at Trent University and doing various odd jobs, he began to write. He is the author of the novel *Life of Pi*, which won the Man Booker Prize in 2002; of *The Facts Behind the Helsinki Roccamatios*, a collection of short stories; and of *Self*, a novel. He lives in Saskatoon.